Portraits of Spiritual Nobility

Portraits of
Spiritual Nobility
Chivalry, Christendom, and
Catholic Culture

TRACEY ROWLAND

Angelico Press

For information, address:
Angelico Press, Ltd.
169 Monitor St.
Brooklyn, NY 11222
www.angelicopress.com

Paper 978-1-62138-446-5
Cloth 978-1-62138-447-2
Ebook 978-1-62138-448-9

Book and cover design
by Michael Schrauzer

In memory of
Rev. Prof. James V. Schall SJ

Habits are, as it were, metaphysical letters patent of nobility, and just as much as inborn talents make for inequality among men, the man with a habit has a quality in him for the lack of which nothing can compensate, as nothing can take its place. Other men are defenceless, he is armor-clad, but his armor is the living armor of the spirit.

— Jacques Maritain, *Art and Scholasticism*

CONTENTS

PREFACE

THE SHORT ESSAYS IN THIS COLLECTION
have been published during the past decade in maga-
zines such as *The Catholic World Report*, the *London
Catholic Herald*, *Crisis Magazine*, *The Catholic Thing*, *Annals
Australasia* and *The Catholic Weekly* of the Archdiocese of Sydney. Some take the form of comment on public events such as
the beatification of John Paul II or the funeral of Archduke Otto
von Hapsburg, others are works of tribute like the reflection
for Pope Benedict's 90th birthday, still others are of a more
personal nature such as the piece entitled "From Rockhampton
to Rome." The latter was an after-dinner address delivered as
part of a series of lectures by lay Catholics reflecting upon the
relationship of their faith to their professional lives.

Certain themes reappear throughout the essays — for example, that liberalism is an ideology hostile to all forms of difference based on standards of excellence; that the Catholic faith
stands on the side of truth, academic excellence, and scholarly
pursuits; that the Catholic faith also stands on the side of beauty
and opposed to all forms of philistinism; that chivalry is an
important element of Catholic culture; and that John Paul II
was one of the most outstanding personalities of the twentieth
century while Joseph Ratzinger/Benedict XVI is a theologian
of "Church Doctor" standing.

Of the many short essays published, the one titled "What's
Wrong with Belgium?" has been a favorite of many readers.
"What's Wrong with Belgium?" is a question often asked by
faithful Catholics. It's the European analogue to "What's Wrong
with Quebec?" In both cases ostensibly Catholic cultures have
imploded in a very short space of time. As a visual symbol of

the tragedy that is the Catholic Church in Belgium, the church of Our Lady of the Sacred Heart and Our Lady of Lourdes, built on the heights of Liege as a war memorial and only completed in 1968, has been deconsecrated and is now up for sale. This is the bitter fruit of half a century of pastoral experiments aimed as correlating the Catholic faith to the *Zeitgeist*.

The collection is dedicated to my very dear friend, Fr James V. Schall SJ, described by many as the "American Chesterton," whose mortal life ended on Wednesday the 17th of April as this book was in the final stages of preparation. The news that Fr Schall was dying broke around the same time as the news that the great Cathedral of Notre Dame de Paris was on fire. In these times one thinks of the line from the Book of Lamentations — *Quomodo sedet sola civitas* — how lonely the city stands.

Tracey Rowland
Holy Week, AD 2019

Nine Centuries of Chivalry

F ROM FEBRUARY 9 TO 15, 2013, THE SOV-
ereign Military Order of St. John of Jerusalem, Rhodes,
and Malta will be celebrating a 900th anniversary.

The Order of Malta, as it is generally known, is the oldest
Order of Chivalry in the world and the fourth oldest religious
Order in the Church. The anniversary marks the date when
Pope Paschal II issued the papal bull *Pie Postulatio Voluntatis*
giving his approval for the foundation of the hospital of St.
John in Jerusalem. The effect of the bull was that those who ran
the hospital became members of a lay religious Order. Today,
the Order of Malta functions as a religious order, an order of
chivalry, and as a sovereign subject of international law. It has
two general missions: the service of the sick and the poor and
the defense of the faith.

At times in its history the defense of the faith took a military
form. In 1565, the Order's Knights defeated a much larger Sar-
acen invading force in the Great Siege of Malta. Their victory
removed the immediate risk of an invasion of Sicily and perhaps,
even more seriously, of the Eternal City herself. Six years later in
the Battle of Lepanto members of the Order contributed three
galleys to the coalition forces which sailed under the name of
the Holy League. Although they were well outnumbered by
the Turkish forces which sailed in a menacing crescent-shaped
configuration, a change in the direction of the wind at the outset
of the naval battle greatly assisted the victory of the Christian
forces. Pius V, the reigning pontiff, attributed the victory to the
intercession of Our Lady to whom whole kingdoms of Christians were then offering rosaries, pleading for her maternal

---

Published in The Catholic Thing, *February 10, 2013.*

protection. It is because of this event that we now have the Feast of Our Lady of the Rosary and the title Our Lady of Victories.

The Order has diplomatic relations with 104 countries and representation at the United Nations and the Parliament of the European Union. It also has 13,500 members and 80,000 permanent volunteers. It is especially active in helping the victims of armed conflicts and natural disasters by the provision of medical aid. It runs general hospitals in Germany, France, England, and Italy, and a maternity hospital in Bethlehem. It also funds medical centers in Benin, Burkina Faso, Cameroon, Madagascar, Togo, and Lebanon. In Senegal and Cambodia the Order has established centers for leprosy sufferers, and AIDS-relief programs are underway in Africa and Central America, with special institutions caring for afflicted mothers and their infants in South Africa and the Philippines.

In the more highly developed countries, palliative care is becoming a key concern for the Order. Catholic patients, understandably, do not want to die in hospitals run on utilitarian principles. They want chapels, not prayer-rooms, crucifixes, not lavender candles, priests with the power to administer sacraments, not social workers with degrees in grief counseling. Lawyers and medical practitioners who are members of the Order are now on the front lines, defending the Christian ethos of medical institutions from the ideologies of the culture of death.

The Order has also founded a Global Fund for Forgotten People. These include people with neglected diseases, children with parents in prison, children born with disabilities, and mothers and newborns without healthcare.

In Madrid and St. Petersburg, the Order operates soup kitchens for the poor and homeless, and in Paris the Order has moored two barges on the Seine River to provide overnight accommodation for homeless men and their dogs. For many of the homeless men, their dog literally is their best friend and not someone from whom they want to be parted at night. The French members of the Order are rather proud of the fact that they have made provision for the dogs.

In this week, therefore, when members of the Order of Malta celebrate 900 years of service to the world, it is worth reflecting on how much we need chivalry.

In popular parlance chivalry is often associated with the practice of a gentleman offering a lady a seat on a peak-hour train or allowing someone older and frailer a safe passage through some other peak-hour scrum. Fundamentally, chivalry is about people with strength and power using whatever gifts they have acquired from nature or education to help those weaker than themselves. It is the complete antithesis of the survival of the fittest principles which govern life among the lower primates.

Feminists tend to be anti-chivalry because they don't like women to be considered the weaker sex — even if weaker in this context means something like "physically less able to move fallen trees and change flat tires," not intellectually slower. Similarly, liberal ideologues don't like chivalry because it suggests that there are actually some people in society who are stronger and more influential than others. The mere existence of such types means that a century of social engineering has failed to bring about the classless utopia.

In contrast, the Christian idea of chivalry simultaneously affirms talent and ability while holding that such talents are best put to use in the one-to-one service of those less able.

Perhaps a stronger affirmation of chivalry in our school's curricula might help overcome a number of social pathologies, including gender ideology, male chauvinism, mindless egalitarianism, and the idea that the service of the sick and the poor and the defense of the faith is something to be achieved by a bureaucracy rather than by real people.

Somewhat paradoxically, the defense of the faith in the 21st century will also entail a defense of chivalry.

2

The Problem Is Bourgeois, Not Aristocratic, Behavior

I N A RECENT *THE CATHOLIC THING* POST, Fr Bevil Bramwell wrote: "Imagine how different the world would be if, for 1,600 years, clergy had chosen to follow the apostolic instead of the aristocratic style."[1]

I would argue that this is a false dichotomy and indeed that the apostolic style is *inherently aristocratic*. The problem is not that we have members of the clergy comporting themselves like aristocrats, but rather that we have members of the clergy comporting themselves like members of the petite bourgeoisie.

The term "aristocratic" originally meant that which is the best or most excellent. It had nothing to do with expensive lunches, hunting foxes, or avoiding contact with the lower orders. It was not a synonym for selfish or snobby.

If we follow the usage of sociologists, there is an "aristocratic" personality type and a "bourgeois" personality type. The hallmarks of the aristocratic are: (1) a strong sense of personal honor and personal responsibility for one's actions, (2) a tendency to place personal honor and integrity above the desire for upward mobility, and (3) a strong belief in the principle that from those to whom much has been given, much will be expected. This is often expressed by the words "*noblesse oblige*," meaning the obligations of the nobility to those less fortunate than themselves.

The bourgeois personality however is associated with giving priority to the goods of efficiency over the goods of excellence,

---

[1] Bevil Bramwell, "Pope Francis and the Hierarchy," *The Catholic Thing*, July 13, 2014.

Written July 2014.

placing economic considerations above all others, and a tendency to tack to and fro with changes in the social wind so as to improve one's chances of upward mobility. The bourgeois type is much more morally flexible than the aristocratic type. The English folk-song *The Vicar of Bray* is a satirical comment on this kind of tacking with changes in the ecclesial breeze.

While some families have a history of breeding offspring with aristocratic dispositions, there is no guarantee that being born into a great family ensures the dispositions, and conversely, one can acquire the dispositions without having been born into a great family. Nonetheless, the history of twentieth-century Catholicism has given us some classic examples of the aristocratic personality type in persons who were actually born into great families.

Prominent twentieth-century examples of the aristocratic type holding episcopal office include: Prince Adam Stefan Sapieha, the Cardinal Archbishop of Kraków who head-hunted a young Karol Wojtyła for the priesthood and protected him in an underground seminary during the war; Blessed Clemens August Graf von Galen, the Lion of Münster, who was described by a British Foreign Office official as "the most outstanding personality among the clergy in the British zone," "statuesque in appearance and uncompromising in discussion," and "[an] oak-bottomed old aristocrat"; and Blessed Baron Vilmos Apor, the Bishop of Győr, who was martyred in 1945 while trying to protect a group of women from being raped by soldiers of the Red Army.

Galen had the audacity to turn up to police stations to complain about the illegality of the Nazi thuggery. He would explain to the police which particular sections of the official criminal code had been violated by the Gestapo. That takes a certain degree of aristocratic panache and fortitude. He also saw off a delegation of Nazi thugs by appearing in complete choir dress with rochet, cappa, cappello, and pectoral cross. The

Nazi officers may not have had any respect for the sanctity of human life, but they could recognize a good uniform. Outside the clergy there are the examples of three of the Hapsburgs: Emperor Karl and his wife Empress Zita, and their eldest son Archduke Otto. John Paul II was actually named "Karol" by his parents, in honor of Emperor Karl in whose army his father served, so it is an extraordinary fact of history that a baby named after an emperor ends up becoming a pope and beatifying the emperor. Even more extraordinary is the fact that their feast days ended up being celebrated on successive days, Blessed Emperor Karl on the 21st of October and St John Paul II on the 22nd of October. The cause for the beatification of Empress Zita has also opened.

Karl and Zita's eldest son, Archduke Otto, displayed something of an aristocratic personality when in his youth he refused several invitations to lunch with Adolf Hitler. Hitler called the Nazi annexation of Austria "Operation Otto" in retaliation for the snubbing. Later in his life, Archduke Otto came to the rescue of John Paul II at a meeting of the European Parliament. During the pope's address to the Parliament, the Reverend Ian Paisley, a Northern Irish Protestant militant, started shouting that the pope was the anti-Christ. Instead of remaining in his seat with the other politicians enjoying the theatre, Archduke Otto ran across the chamber and helped the security guards to remove the ranting Orangeman.

What all of these people have in common is that they are not afraid to lead, they are not afraid to stand out from the crowd, they don't put their own personal safety and comfort above their social responsibilities, they have a low tolerance of idiots and thugs and a "not on my watch" attitude toward evil practices. Alternatively, the idea that "I can't stand against the system," or that it isn't my responsibility, or that I can delegate this challenge to a committee or a lawyer, or stand behind the authority of the bureaucracy, is typical of the petite bourgeois mentality of the generation of bishops who covered up child abuse.

Edmund Burke is famous for his statement that the only thing that evil needs in order to triumph is for good men to do nothing.

Pope Francis is famous for his metaphor about the clergy needing to smell like their sheep. This metaphor was greeted with mixed reactions in countries like Australia and New Zealand where there are literally tens of millions of four-legged sheep who don't smell all that well. Australian Catholics and Kiwi Catholics would be repelled by clergy smelling like sheep. Nonetheless, the faithful do want shepherds who will suffer for them and put their very lives on the line to protect them. They don't want people who treat the priesthood as a career.

My point is simply that careerism is not an aristocratic lifestyle option at all.

3

What's Wrong with Belgium?
Lament for a Once-Catholic Nation

T HERE IS SOMETHING BEAUTIFUL ABOUT Belgium if one thinks of the Flemish architecture, the canals, the countryside dotted with grayish-blue cows, the coffee served with whipped cream (in Flemish *Slagroom*) in the cafes and patisseries. There are country lanes with bicycles and villages with medieval churches and towns with great works of Christian art. There's Van Eyck's *Adoration of the Lamb* and the venerated relic of Holy Blood allegedly collected by Joseph of Arimathea and brought from the Holy Land by Thierry of Alsace, Count of Flanders. However, against all this natural beauty and fine works of art, including the artistic works of the pastry chefs and the lace-makers, there is something deeply sinister about this country. Its Catholic culture has been trashed by a couple of generations of intellectuals at war with their own heritage.

I first visited Belgium in 2004 to attend a theology conference in Leuven. The conference Mass was quite bizarre. It did not take place in any of the many churches in Leuven but in the conference room itself. Part of the ritual took the form of watching a video of the September 11 attack on the Twin Towers while listening to mood music. One of the participants from Holland was constantly dressed in a folk costume. He looked like a member of the band *The Village People*. There was also a Nigerian priest who was treated like an idiot because he expressed respect for Cardinal Arinze. I took some flak for being critical of the culture of modernity and one polite person

Published in Crisis Magazine, *February 18, 2014.*

apologized to me by saying, "you see, around here people think of you as an ally of Joseph Ratzinger"!

My overall impression was that Leuven was like a town that had been hit by a neutron bomb — the kind of bomb that kills people but leaves buildings intact. All the Gothic buildings remained, and the outward symbols of a once vibrant Catholic culture were still on view as tourist attractions; but the people who worked within the buildings were at war with this heritage.

A few years later I attended another theology conference, this time in Kraków. A Belgian Professor delivered the key-note address in the hall of the Polish Academy of the Arts and Sciences. He veered off topic and gave a rousing oration in favor of each of the projects of the culture of death (eugenics, euthanasia, and not merely contraception but a tax on babies). He even argued that anyone who opposed contraception should be convicted of a criminal offence. Not all the conference partic-ipants were against contraception, indeed there were quite a few Anglicans present for whom contraception is not a moral issue at all. However, the participants, including the non-Catholics, were completely shocked that such an anti-life and totalitarian speech could be given in the hall of the Polish Academy just a couple of hours' drive from Auschwitz. What stunned the participants was the closeness of the ideology of the speaker to that of the Nazi ideologues whose specters (metaphorically speaking) still haunt the streets of Kraków.

A quick Google search revealed that the illustrious academic had been Jesuit educated in Antwerp and was a product of the University of Leuven. A more recent Google search revealed that last year he ended his life by receiving a lethal injection. He at least had the virtue of practicing what he preached, but I wondered how someone who was Jesuit-educated in the 1930s could end up in such a spiritual state. In an interview given not long before his death, he said that religion is nonsense, a childish explanation for things that science has yet to fathom. At some moment in his life he had accepted some version of Feuerbach's belief that Christianity is at best a psychological crutch.

In addition to making the occasional visit to Belgium's universities, every year I watch the Eurovision Song Contest. Even if the music ranges from the pathetic to the completely comical, with much in between, Eurovision throws up interesting cultural epiphenomena. Last year one of the worst songs in the entire contest was the entry from Belgium. It was called "Love Kills." The refrain was: "Waiting for the bitter pill/Give me something I can feel/Cause love kills over and over/Love kills over and over."

Whatever this means exactly, it's a radical inversion of the normal juxtaposition of love with life and generativity. Other countries offered the usual assortment of Eurovision styles, some heavy metal, some punk, a few soft ballads, but the Belgian entry stood out as something dark and depressive. It was perhaps the very first culture of death pop song.

Poor King Philippe is now in a position of having to decide what to do about the fact that his government has voted in favor of euthanasia for children. Many hope that he will follow the precedent of his saintly uncle King Baudouin who in 1990 abdicated for a day rather than have his name attached to pro-abortion legislation. At the time King Baudouin rhetorically asked: Is it right that I am the only Belgian citizen to be forced to act against his conscience in such a crucial area? Is the freedom of conscience sacred for everyone except for the king?

The hospital in Brussels where sick children are to be "put down" is named in honor of Queen Fabiola, the widow of King Baudouin. She is a devout Catholic. Presumably she doesn't want her name associated with an institution that gives lethal injections to children. Perhaps she will withdraw permission for the use of her name from the hospital?

What went wrong? How can a nation that is even nominally Catholic do this? Can all this be pinned on the theology of Edward Schillebeeckx and his colleagues who wanted to correlate theology to the spirit of the times, to accommodate Catholicism to modernity? Or is the causality much more complex? Why is Belgium in so much worse a state than France or even Germany?

In the wake of this parliamentary decision, bloggers from across the English Channel are suggesting that the British defense of Belgium in World War I was a huge mistake. If the Belgians really desire a culture of death they could have settled for Prussian domination a century earlier and saved the rest of the world a whole lot of trauma.

King Baudouin and Queen Fabiola may not have been able to protect the Catholic culture of Belgium from the *Zeitgeist* of the 1960s but at least they took an unambiguous stand against it. Some battles can't be won politically, only spiritually, and sometimes the political victories follow decades and even centuries of spiritual preparation. For example, historians now say that the decade of the Great Polish Novena (from the mid-50s to the mid-60s) was the spiritual, intellectual, and even logistical preparation for the emergence of the Polish Solidarity movement in the 1980s.

The current predicament in which King Philippe finds himself is but another moment in a battle which began sometime in the 1960s when Belgian intellectuals decided that the Catholic faith is something you make up for yourself, rather than something you receive. Let's pray that King Philippe has the courage to stand in solidarity with his late uncle, and all those throughout the world who believe that human life is sacred. Let's hope that he looks at this crisis from the perspective of eternity.

4

Europe Farewells a Catholic Hero

FRANZ JOSEF OTTO ROBERT MARIA ANTON Karl Max Heinrich Sixtus Xavier Felix Renatus Ludwig Gaetan Pius Ignatius von Habsburg-Lothringen (normally known as Archduke or Dr Otto von Habsburg) passed away at his home in Bavaria on July 4, 2011, at the age of 98.

He was the eldest son of Emperor Karl and Empress Zita von Hapsburg-Lothringen and, as such, would have been the Emperor of Austria and King of Hungary, were it not for the treasonous behavior of various forces at the end of the First World War that led to his family's exile.

His father Karl was beatified by Pope John Paul II in 2004, and the cause for his mother's beatification was opened in 2009.

The years of Archduke Otto's childhood were difficult because of his family's exile and poverty and the death of his father when he was only nine years old. Nonetheless, his mother saw to it that he received the education of a prince. He learned to speak German, Hungarian, French, English, Spanish, and Croatian, as well as reading classical Greek and Latin.

In the winter of 1931–1932 Adolf Hitler twice invited the young Archduke to luncheon but on both occasions the invitation was declined. Otto had read *Mein Kampf* and concluded that Hitler was not the kind of person with whom he wanted any association. When the German army invaded Austria in 1938 Hitler named the invasion 'Operation Otto' to humiliate the Hapsburgs and in 1941 Hitler personally declared that members of the Hapsburg family could no longer be regarded as citizens of Austria. The Gestapo were under orders to execute Otto if he was found.

Published in Kairos, *August 5, 2011.*

After the Second World War Archduke Otto made a living as a journalist and professional public speaker, having acquired a doctorate in political and social sciences from the University of Louvain. In 1950 he met his wife Princess Regina of Saxe-Meiningen who was herself a refugee and the daughter of Prince Georg of Saxe-Meiningen and Countess Klara-Marie von Korff genannt Schmissing-Kerssenbrock. Her father died in a Russian prisoner-of-war camp at Cherepovets a year after the Second World War ended when she was only 21. They established their family home in Bavaria and together raised a family of seven children, which grew to include 22 grandchildren and two great-grandchildren.

In 1979 Otto entered the European Parliament as a Christian Social Union representative for North Bavaria and retained that position for the next twenty years.

When John Paul II addressed the European Parliament in 1988, the member for Northern Ireland, the Rev. Ian Paisley, internationally renowned for anti-Catholic rhetoric, stood up and shouted that John Paul II was the anti-Christ and unfurled a banner to this effect. Archduke Otto ran to Paisley, pulled down the banner and, with the help of a few security guards, escorted Paisley out of the chamber.

A year later as European Communism was beginning to implode the Archduke organized a Pan-European Picnic on the border of Hungary and Austria which helped some seven hundred East Germans to escape to the West. In the historical accounts of the fall of Communism, the Pan-European Picnic is now regarded as one of the significant events that led to the destruction of the Berlin Wall.

These are just sample illustrations of the hundreds of good projects fostered by the Archduke throughout his lifetime. He had worked hard to keep Austria out of the clutches of Hitler and when that failed and Hungary fell into the Communist zone, he spent several decades helping Europeans caught on the wrong side of the Iron Curtain. Throughout his life he championed the idea of a European Union built on solid Christian cultural foundations.

Some 100,000 people lined the streets of Vienna on the day of his funeral over which Cardinal Schönborn presided as Pope Benedict's official delegate. The coffin was draped with the Hapsburg arms pall and guided by a guard of Tyrolean musketeers. All the major chivalric and religious orders processed behind the coffin which took the historic route past the Hofburg, as with the funeral of Emperor Franz Joseph in 1916.

The Mass setting was the C-minor Requiem of Haydn and the traditional Habsburg burial rite was followed. When the coffin reaches the door of the Capuchin crypt, a friar asks the name of the deceased and then all the Christian names and royal titles are solemnly read. The friar then says that he has never heard of the person. Only at the response "it's a poor sinner" does the friar open the door. In this instance on the second call, Archduke Otto's political achievements were recited before the Chamberlain got to the "he's just a poor sinner" bit of the ritual.

Europe has lost a Catholic hero.

5

Christophobia and the
Ideologues of Liberal Democracy

RYSZARD LEGUTKO IS NOT ALL THAT well known in Anglophone circles but he is a huge name in Poland. In the 1980s he was a young academic in Kraków writing books and articles about political theory for the underground publishers.

In the post-Communist era he has served as the Minister of Education, Secretary of State in the Chancellery of the late President Lech Kaczynski, and Deputy Speaker of the Polish Senate. He is currently a member of the European Parliament and Deputy Chairman of the Parliamentary Group of European Conservatives and Reformists. He is also a professor of philosophy at Poland's most prestigious university—the Jagiellonian—founded in 1364 by Casimir the Great and the alma mater of St John Paul II. Legutko's English publications include *Society as a Department Store: Critical Reflections on the Liberal State* (2002) and *The Demon in Democracy: Totalitarian Temptations in Free Societies* (2016).

This most recent work addresses a theme close to the heart of many Poles of the heroic Solidarity generation, namely, why was it that Communists found it so easy to transform themselves into Liberal Democrats while retaining their hostility to the Catholic Church and the Catholic family as social institutions?

In the watershed year of 1989, the Communists and leaders of the anti-Communist opposition cut a deal. Certain government positions were transferred to the anti-Communists and free elections followed, but there were to be no retributions,

Published in the Catholic World Report, *February 27, 2017.*

no punishment for the Communist criminals, nothing like a Nuremburg trial for the former Communist high officials.

In 1989 this was thought to be the most prudent course of action. No one wanted a Soviet invasion of Poland and its accompanying brutality. However, the end result is that today, to quote a Polish friend, "people who had their teeth kicked out by Communists in the 1980s are now driving taxis to make a living, while the same Communists are retired on state pensions."

Legutko's latest book, *The Demon in Democracy*, offers an explanation for this tragic state of affairs as well as a penetrating analysis of the folly of Christian elites who pursue policies of assimilation with the *Zeitgeist* of Liberal Democracy.

While Legutko acknowledges that Liberal Democracy is not as bad as Communism, and indeed for as long as the practitioners of Liberal Democracy were predominately of a Judeo-Christian mindset, it was vastly superior to Communism, he nonetheless argues that both Communism and Liberal Democracy currently share the same hostility to Christianity and the same propensity for totalitarian behavior.

First, the Communist and Liberal Democratic ideologies share a perception of history as developing according to a linear pattern. For the Communists the dynamic of human history is the class struggle, for the Liberal Democrats the dynamic is a social struggle between the team of freedom and the team of authority. Since the Church plays for the team of authority, it always finds itself on the wrong side of Liberal Democratic ideology.

Secondly, Communists and Liberal Democrats agree that the future utopian order requires the preliminary agency of enlightened freedom fighters, for example, the work of partisan journalists and intellectuals. Often the only opposition to both groups is found within the small milieu of Catholic scholars.

Thirdly, Communists and Liberal Democrats agree that in their new world order people will be liberated from all forms of superstition and ignorance. Since Christianity requires faith in revelation it is deemed to be the greatest purveyor of superstition and ignorance and thus the institution most in need of social marginalization.

There is, moreover, an attitude common to Communists and Liberal Democrats that the political system should permeate every section of public and private life. Not only should the economy be liberal, but the Church and the family, schools and universities, and indeed, culture itself should be democratic. No distinctions are to be made between ballet and rap dancing, opera and hip hop, tabloid journalism and meticulous scholarship, happy families and unhappy families, casual hook-ups and life-long relationships. All forms of aristocratic culture (that is, cultures built upon an acknowledgement of different grades of excellence and authority) need to be eradicated. To assist this, the entertainment industry encourages what Legutko (following Pascal) calls *divertissement*— activity that separates people from the seriousness of existence and fills this existence with cheap and shallow content.

As Legutko expresses the principle, "for the ideologues of liberal democracy it is necessary to intervene deeply into the social substance — where the roots of status and recognition reside — either through direct political action or indirectly by changing the laws, making appropriate judicial decisions, and adjusting morality and social mores drastically to guarantee equality."[1] Hence, "literature, art, education, family, liturgy, the Bible, traditions, ideas, entertainment and even children's toys" are all areas of private life which have been deemed to require state intervention for the sake of a common democratic cultural order. Most often it is the Education Departments of governments which set up bureaucracies to police these fields.

[1] Ryszard Legutko, *The Demon in Democracy: Totalitarian Temptations in Free Societies* (Encounter Books, 2016), 62.

Legutko argues that the Liberal-Democratic man has politicized his privacy, his marriage, his family relations, his communal life and language, and in these efforts he resembles his Communist comrade. But his greatest success, which goes beyond anything achieved by the Old Left Communists, is to politicize the realm of sex itself. The English sociologist Anthony Giddens has called this "the democratization of intimacy."[2]

While the old-style Marxists had only "class" as an ideological leverage, the ideological trend of contemporary Liberal-Democratic ideologues is "class, race, and gender."

Legutko also observes that those contaminated by ideology develop a deep suspicion towards ideas. They want to dismiss intellectual judgments as the epiphenomena of class interest (Marx) or weakness of the body (Nietzsche) or an unresolved Oedipus complex (Freud).

The universities were traditionally havens of aristocratic culture but they have become so thoroughly democratized they now resemble businesses. As Legutko notes, "the functioning of the university itself has become so heavily controlled by procedures, rules and regulations that all deviations from the routine are strictly controlled."

Legutko concludes that the European Union has become "the guardian of all diseases of the supranational Liberal Democracy while itself being the most vivid illustration of these diseases." Whereas the early Liberal intellectuals — Grotius and Kant, for example — merely desired a social order without war, the generation of '68 intellectuals who created the Union of Maastricht want to create a European demos and a new European man.

Legutko accuses the European Union of "Christophobia." He concludes that the vulgarity of the Communist system was pre-cultural while that of Liberal Democracy is post-cultural.

---

[2] Anthony Giddens, *The Transformation of Intimacy: Sexuality, Love and Eroticism in Modern Societies* (Stanford University Press, 1993).

The scary thing about this analysis is that the only institution potentially strong enough to stand in the way of a new age of barbarism is the Catholic Church. Yet here Legutko observes a parallel between today's clerical leaders who want to accommodate the Church to the culture of Liberal Democracy and those Catholic leaders in the 1950s and 60s who thought they could defend the Church by making concessions to the Communists.

The historical record shows that the Poles defeated the Communists, not by making concessions, but by resisting the Communists in both thought and practice, and ultimately, in producing a scholar-saint of exceptional moral and intellectual authority who led a whole generation.

6

Open Wide the Doors to Christ

KAROL WOJTYŁA WAS BEATIFIED IN Rome on the 1st of May which, in 2011 in the Catholic calendar, was both Divine Mercy Sunday and the Feast of St. Joseph the Worker. May 1st is also the highest of holy days for Communists who still exist, albeit in dwindling numbers, in Italy.

As a Dean of one of the eight John Paul II Institutes worldwide, I was in Rome for the ceremony. I started to make my way to St. Peter's Basilica around 7 am for a 10 am Mass. I caught a train from the Manzoni Metro to Ottaviani, which is about a ten-minute trip. In my carriage sitting opposite was a lady carrying a beatification booklet. As our train crossed the Tiber she became quite animated. I looked around to see if there was something in the river that may have been responsible for her reaction, like a papal barge or some such thing, but there was nothing. I smiled at her as if to say, okay, I understand, it is a sacred moment, we are crossing the Tiber. She smiled back and asked in Italian if I was attending the beatification ceremony. I said *Si* and then to indicate that my Italian is a work in progress—*Sono Australian*. She then switched to English and asked if it was my first trip to Rome. I said No, I work for a John Paul II Institute, so I come over once a year. At the mention of the words "John Paul II Institute" she changed seats, sat beside me, and kissed me on both cheeks, European style. She then extended her hand and said, "I am Elena, from Milano." She added that she was a cardiology nurse.

At this moment my thoughts went back to another Roman experience when I was approached by a young man who said

Published in Kairos, *May 5, 2011.*

that his name was Jorge and that he came from Peru and was a member of a new ecclesial movement whose leader wanted to meet me. I said "Sure," gave him my hotel details, and agreed to be collected for dinner at a certain time. As I waited to be collected it occurred to me that he could be an axe-murderer for all I knew. I didn't even know his surname. He did however turn out to be telling the truth.

I decided that this was a Jorge type of Roman experience and I became instant friends with Elena. She asked if I would like to join her and her priest friend Don Battista. I agreed and the three of us set off for St. Peter's. We got about half way along the road that runs from the Ottaviani Metro to St. Peter's when the police turned us back. There was no more room anywhere along the Via Conciliazione which stretches from the Basilica all the way to the Tiber. It was jam packed with some 1.5 million people. Crowds had been arriving since two in the morning.

The police suggested that we retreat to the Lateran Basilica where plasma screens had been set up to cope with the overflow. We walked back to the Metro and found ourselves in a human traffic snarl. Thousands of people were still pouring out of the Metro while thousands of others had been turned back by police and were heading into the Metro. There were so many people it was not possible to get anywhere near the ticket machines. The only hope was to queue for human service, but these queues were about 30 people deep. Just as I was concluding that I would spend the ceremony stuck in an underground metro, Elena again became animated. She had noticed a friend at the head of one of the queues. She called out "Luciano, Luciano," and then instructions for three more tickets. Luciano got the message and emerged from the scrum with a ticket for me, Elena, and Don Battista. There was no time to exchange money, so I thanked the complete stranger for buying my ticket and when we finally got onto a train Elena said "Luciano is a psychologist," and then to Luciano, "Tracey is an Australian theologian."

It occurred to me that this was something of a foretaste of the end of the world. Leaving aside the fear and trembling, this was a moment when all the sheep were gathered together in the one place, and all feeling close and friendly, because, regardless of whether or not we could speak each other's language, we were united by a bond that was so deep it didn't need to be expressed in any language. The gestures, like Luciano's ticket for me, or his bow in my direction as he stood back and let me off the train first, were enough.

I tried to explain to Elena that I thought it was like the end of the world, but she didn't understand "end of world." I tried words like consummation and eschaton, but they didn't help. She suggested French and I countered with German. She agreed to German. I then said: "Es ist wie das Ende der Zeit wenn Christ gekommen will." She didn't get it but gave me a hug as a compensatory gesture.

We got to the Lateran in time for the start of the ceremony. The crowd broke into applause as Pope Benedict appeared. He was looking relaxed and happy. A nun then brought forward the vial of blood which was taken from John Paul II before his death. As she came forward the choir chanted a motet in Latin. Don Battista had come with the whole Order of Service and allowed me to read the words of the hymn over his shoulder. The translation was "Open Wide the Doors to Christ." As the Pope read out the decree of beatification an icon of John Paul II was unveiled behind the sanctuary.

In his homily Pope Benedict spoke of John Paul II's experiences in Communist Poland and how these led him to conclude that the contemporary culture wars are over what it means to be human. John Paul II wanted to juxtapose the Marxist idea of the human person with the Christian. This was evident in the very first lines of his first encyclical *Redemptor Hominis*. Whereas the first sentence of Karl Marx's *Communist Manifesto* was "Workers of the World Unite, the history of the world is the history of class conflict," the first sentence of *Redemptor Hominis* was "Jesus Christ, the Redeemer of Man, is the center and purpose of human history." For one, class conflict and economics is the dynamic of history, for the other it is Christ. Pope Benedict emphasized that the pontificate of John Paul II was all about the promotion of a Christian anthropology. He noted that this anthropology is found in the documents of the Second Vatican Council and that John Paul II, who attended the Council as a bishop, is an authentic interpreter of the meaning of the Council.

Toward the end of the Mass those of us who were watching on the Lateran's plasma screen were escorted into the Lateran Basilica to receive Holy Communion. We returned to the square in time for the Regina Caeli and final blessing. I then said farewell to my new friends, exchanged addresses, and promised them all free bed and breakfast if they ever visit Melbourne.

On my way to my hotel I passed one of the May 1st Communist demonstrations. About 50 young people were carrying "ban the bomb" posters and Soviet flags. I had not seen a Soviet flag for decades. They were marching directly against a crowd of Poles. The red and white flags of the Poles merged with the red and yellow flags of the Communists. I watched to see if there would be a confrontation but the Poles were too happy to even notice their archenemies.

Other standout memories of the day included the sight of huge signs on the doors of restaurants and bars around St. Peter's bearing the words "NO TOILET," a scene on a train where two obviously homosexual Italians were the subject of a morals lecture by a Polish lady (she spoke in Polish, they countered in Italian), a couple of scenes of bishops and monsignori pleading with police to allow them access to roads around the

Vatican which had been blocked off, and best of all, T-shirts with the words "Tu es Christ" under a smiling image of John Paul II. Of course, the correct Latin is *Tu es Christus*, but leaving aside the problem of spelling, the fact is that John Paul II was the pope, not Christ. It should have been "Tu es Petrus." Lucky there were no Protestants anywhere to be scandalized.

When it came to sartorial sensibilities, the prize for the best dressed, as always, went to the French, while the prize for the most theatrical regalia went to a group operating on the Vittorio Emanuele bridge. They were wearing long red capes with a huge image of Christ the King printed on the red cloth. They had covered the bridge with banners. One said, "1 million angels for Benedict XVI," another, "Free Rome: Ultramontanism." They were walking about the bridge handing out holy cards and miraculous medals. I tried to find one who could speak enough English to explain who they were but they were not very good at English and I ended up with several holy cards and miraculous medals but no deeper understanding.

My dominant spiritual impression was that these crowds of 1.5–2 million were a concrete example of what the French novelist Georges Bernanos had written about spiritual childhood. Bernanos thought that the best parts of the human being are those elements of faith and hope which somehow manage to survive childhood and do not get snuffed out by the brutality of the adult world. J. K. Rowling was onto a similar insight with her concept of dementors. In the *Harry Potter* books, dementors are monsters who operate by sucking the hope out of people. It occurred to me that for a few hours at least, Rome was a dementor-free zone. Catholics could find sheer unadulterated joy in being Catholics. It was as if everyone had rediscovered the joy of children, the traffic jams notwithstanding.

All 1.5–2 million had their parts to play in a theo-drama much larger than any individual. There was a sense that together they could actually achieve what John Paul II wanted, which is to turn the trajectory of Western civilization away from a culture of death to a civilization of love. I imagined that in heaven they will all tell stories, like old soldiers, of how they did their bit. There would be stories of this battle, that fight, those particular dementors, the angelic assistance, the prayers of the saints, the friendships forged along the way. I also imagined that at the end of time, Christ will not put the Italian police in charge of traffic management, but if he does, I will be relying on Elena, Luciano, and Don Battista to shepherd me through.

7

John Paul II:
A Brother in Arms
through Baptisms of Fire

B Y ANY STANDARD KAROL WOJTYŁA WAS
one of the most extraordinary world leaders of the 20th
century. He was a published poet and playwright, a
distinguished professor of philosophy, a father of the Second
Vatican Council, a thorn in the side of the Polish Communist
government, the author of significant theological works on the
meaning and purpose of human sexuality and human labor, a
pope who helped to bring an end to European Communism
through a strategy of non-violent solidarity, the survivor of an
assassination attempt, a friend of Mother Teresa, a proponent
of St Faustina's spirituality of Divine Mercy, and a man with
a strong Marian spirituality including a special interest in the
theological significance of the Fatima messages. He studied
twelve languages and was generally renowned for his com-
munication skills. Through his very public death he taught
people how to die with dignity. Last, but not least, he was the
founder of an international network of John Paul II Institutes
for Marriage and Family Studies.

Wojtyła is also possibly the most famous son of Poland ever.
Not even Copernicus and Chopin can match him in terms of the
number of airports, bridges, hospitals, schools, kindergartens,
universities, cultural centers, avenues, and boulevards named
in his honor. Even the Polish version of a vanilla slice has taken
on his name at cafes on the John Paul II cultural tourism trails.

Published in Kairos, *April 27, 2014.*

Outside of Poland there are also numerous public places named for him, including a soccer stadium in Brazil and a peninsula in Antarctica.

The closest I ever got to meeting him was a moment in Sydney in 1995. I was part of a crowd of people who stood outside St. Mary's Cathedral after the beatification ceremony for Mary MacKillop who is now Australia's first and only saint. We sang hymns and folk songs for about an hour until he came out onto the balcony of the presbytery. He began his conversation with us by saying: "How come I can hear you without microphone but you can't hear me without microphone?" [Poles don't use definite articles like "a" or "the"]. We couldn't verbally respond to that but we did fall on our knees much to the amusement of the police. I think we were the most well behaved bunch of "celebrity fans" the police had ever encountered. The Pope then started to ask questions which only required a Yes or No answer. Three times he asked, "Are you for me, are you for Christ?" Each time we screamed "Yes." After the third time he replied, "then come with me to Sri Lanka." (The way that this mirrored Christ's thrice-asked question to St. Peter was not lost on any of us.) He went on to talk about his forthcoming trip to Sri Lanka and he asked us to pray for him. This is what he meant by "come with me to Sri Lanka." He then blessed us and went back inside to his dinner with the bishops. A priest then came out and said: "Okay, we have heard enough Salve Reginas" and politely suggested that we leave the precinct, which we did. Later at a restaurant we all agreed that we would abandon our jobs and get on a plane and go to Sri Lanka if he really wanted that.

Thus, the question arises, why did so many love him? What made him great? Was it just that he was bright, multilingual, and a good communicator?

My first thought is that he was an alpha male who was

integrated. By alpha male I mean he was a natural born leader. If he wasn't the Cardinal Archbishop of Kraków he may well have been the mayor of Kraków or Vice-Chancellor of the Jagiellonian University. By integrated I mean his head and heart worked in tandem. He was the type of leader who could work simultaneously on the intellectual and affective levels. He could exude affection and appreciate the uniqueness of each person he met at the same time as being intellectually sharp. He was an example of what a human person could be if grace was allowed to get to work on nature.

Like alpha male lions he was brave. He never sat in his office and retreated into some safe "other world" while his sheep were suffering outside his door. When families were dysfunctional as a secondary effect of two World Wars and Communism, he set up a clinic and staffed it with professional psychologists to help them. When the youth in his university circle struggled with aspects of sexual maturity he sought to understand their problems and developed a whole theology of the body, reforming the pastoral responses in this area. When Communists tried to stop churches being built he consecrated new building sites, risking his own imprisonment. He even said Mass out in the open, in the rain, to defy them.

No doubt he meant different things to different people. For the peoples of Central Europe he was a liberator, for priests unsure of the value of their vocation he affirmed the importance of the sacramental presence of Christ, for married couples he affirmed the dignity of their sacramental bond and their role in creating a civilization of love, for scholars he demonstrated how one can be both Catholic and reasonable.

A very popular song in Poland in the 1980s was Dire Straits' *Brothers in Arms*. It included the lines: "Through these fields of destruction / Baptisms of fire / I've witnessed all your suffering / As the battle raged higher / And though they did hurt me so bad / In the fear and alarm / You did not desert me / My brothers in arms."

This song was played over and over in the central square of Kraków in the summer of 1989. For faithful Catholics everywhere John Paul II was a brother in arms. He shared in their sufferings and never went to ground in the midst of the battle. He had leonine courage and a heart and intellect to match. He was chivalrous!

8

Karol Wojtyła on Cultural and Spiritual Capital as the Foundation of Freedom and Independence

YOUR EMINENCE, CARDINAL DZIWISZ, Your Excellency, Archbishop Jędraszewski, distinguished faculty and students of the great Jagiellonian University and civic leaders of the city of Kraków, I am deeply honored to accept your invitation to speak today to celebrate the centenary of Poland's independence in 2018 and to recall the many contributions made by your alumnus, Karol Wojtyła, to the defense of that independence.

The specific argument I would like to make is that for Wojtyła, and many other famous Polish patriots, the foundation of freedom and independence is cultural and spiritual capital. Of course, it helps to have financial strength, as the United States has financial strength, and it helps to have an experienced military class. It's hard to imagine the British empire without the British navy, or the rise of the Iberian nations without seafarers like Henry the Navigator. I am not suggesting that financial capital and military power are not important, but I would argue that Poland's independence and freedom rests ultimately upon her cultural and spiritual capital.

In the era of Solidarność, which at least some of you will remember, the slogan chanted across the free world was "Let Poland be Poland," *Niech Polska będzie Polską.* Such a slogan would make no sense unless it was clear to all what Poland is.

Delivered on November 8, 2018 in Kraków, Poland.

For Karol Wojtyła, Poland was something more than a geographical or political construct. It was a cultural and spiritual reality rooted in the graces of the Incarnation. In his address to a meeting of UNESCO leaders in 1980, John Paul II said:

> I am the son of a nation which has lived the greatest experiences of history, which its neighbors have condemned to death several times, but which has survived and remained itself. It has kept its identity, and it has kept, in spite of partitions and foreign occupations, its national sovereignty, not by relying on the resources of physical power, but solely by relying on its culture. This culture turned out in the circumstances to be more powerful than all other forces.

In a later reflection published in 2005 under the title *Memory and Identity,* John Paul II spoke extensively about what he saw as the building blocks of Polish culture and especially the achievements of Polish culture during the period of the partitions in the nineteenth century. He began with the following observation:

> It is well known that the nineteenth century marked a high point in Polish culture. Never before had the Polish nation produced writers of such genius as Adam Mackiewicz, Juliusz Słowacki, Zygmunt Krasiński, or Cyprian Norwid. Polish music had never before reached such heights as in the works of Fryderyk Chopin, Stanisław Moniuszko and other composers . . . the same can be said of painting and sculpture. The nineteenth century is the century of Jan Matejko and Artur Grottger; at the turn of the

century Stanisław Wyspiański appears on the scene, an extraordinary genius in several fields, followed by Jacek Malczewski and others...

At the end of this inventory of the cultural capital of nineteenth-century Poland, Wojtyła concluded with the following statement:

> It must be said that this same period of extraordinary cultural maturity during the nineteenth century fortified the Poles for the great struggle which led the nation to regain its independence. Poland having been struck off the map of Europe, reappeared in 1918 and has remained there ever since. Not even the insane storm of hate unleashed from East and West between 1939 and 1945 could destroy it.[1]

Many books have been written about the renaissance of Polish literature and music in the 19th century and of the Polish regard for what people call the Republic of Letters, that is, the place of scholars and artists in public life, and the general high value that Poles give to education. In the 19th century the English writer Daniel Defoe remarked that it doesn't matter if one can't speak Polish since it's possible to get around Poland quite easily with Latin. The French have a whole quarter of Paris designated as the Latin quarter where the intellectuals live, but according to Defoe, in the nineteenth century, "anyone who knows Latin can easily travel across the whole of Poland from one side to the other."

It is the case that most of the great universities of the world were founded either by popes, bishops, or kings. It is also

---

[1]   Karol Wojtyla, *Memory and Identity* (London: Phoenix, 2005), 67.

interesting to note that over the centuries at least 74 kings and queens have been canonized as saints. However, as far as I can tell, only Poland has produced a saintly queen who gave away all her worldly wealth to establish a university. Poland is also the only country to have the phenomenon of "flying universities."

As you probably all know, the first flying university was started by women in Warsaw in 1882. One of its graduates was Marie Skłodowska-Curie, who discovered the elements radium and polonium, which provided a major breakthrough in the treatment of cancer. Marie Skłodowska-Curie became the first female professor of the University of Paris and the first person to receive two Nobel Prizes: one in physics and one in chemistry. The flying university of the 19th century kept alive the cultural capital of a partitioned Poland and made sure that Poland was not without an educated social class.

During World War II both the Nazis and the Soviet Communists pursued a deliberate policy of decapitating Polish society. The Soviets sought to destroy the officer class in places like Katyn while the Nazis murdered some 600 Polish professors and some 9,000 school teachers, among their other victims. Again a flying university went into operation. Historians claim that around 100,000 Poles were educated during the Nazi occupation by lecturers attached to the flying universities. Alumni of the WWII flying university generation included the poet Zbigniew Herbert and the poet, philosopher, priest and pope, Karol Wojtyła. Wojtyła was also involved in an underground theatre operation.

As you know from sad experience, after the Nazis left the Communists moved in, and so in 1956 the flying university was up and running again. It was ultimately through the work of the flying university in this era that a generation of anti-Communist dissident intellectuals was able to be educated free from the indoctrination of Marxist ideology.

The importance of cultural capital for Karol Wojtyła was such that it formed the central theme of his address at Victory Square in Warsaw during his first trip to his homeland as pope, on June 2, 1979. In this address he stated:

> The history of the nation deserves to be adequately appraised in the light of its contribution *to the development of man and humanity,* to intellect, heart and conscience. This is the deepest stream of culture. It is culture's firmest support, its core, its strength.

He then went on to add:

> It is . . . *impossible without Christ to understand the history of the Polish nation* — this great thousand-year-old community — that is so profoundly decisive for me and each one of us. If we reject this key to understanding our nation, we lay ourselves open to a substantial misunderstanding. We no longer understand ourselves. It is impossible without Christ to understand this nation with its past so full of splendor and also of terrible difficulties. It is impossible to understand this city, Warsaw, the capital of Poland, that undertook in 1944 an unequal battle against the aggressor, a battle in which it was abandoned by the Allied powers, a battle in which it was buried under its own ruins — if it is not remembered that under those same ruins there was also the statue of Christ the Savior with his Cross [that today stands] in front of the church at Krakowskie Przedmieście. It is impossible to understand the history of Poland from Stanislaus in Skalka to Maximilian Kolbe at Oswiecim unless we apply to them that same single *fundamental criterion* that is called Jesus Christ.

37

One day later, in his Address to Young People at Gniezo, John Paul II again reiterated the importance of cultural capital. He described culture as an "expression of man" and a "confirmation of humanity," and a "common good of the nation." Moreover, he argued:

> Polish culture is a good on which the spiritual life of Poles rests. It distinguishes [Polish people] as a nation. It is decisive for us throughout the course of history, more decisive even than material power. Indeed, it is more decisive than political boundaries. The Polish nation, as is well known, passed through the hard trial of the loss of its independence for over a hundred years. And in the midst of this trial it preserved its own identity. *It remained spiritually independent because it had its own culture.* Indeed, in the period of the partitions it still greatly enriched its culture and made it deeper, since it is only by creating culture that it can keep itself in being.

Having again made the point that Polish independence is linked to Poland's cultural capital, John Paul II, following the pattern of his Victory Square Address, then linked Polish cultural capital to Poland's Christocentric spiritual capital. He noted that:

> Polish culture still flows with a broad stream of inspirations that have their source in the Gospel. This contributes also to *the deeply humanistic character of this culture.* It makes it so deeply and authentically human, since, as Adam Mickiewicz wrote in his *Księgi Narodu i Pielgrzymstwa Polskiego,* "a civilization truly worthy of man must be a Christian civilization."

John Paul II concluded his address to the youth by saying:

> You are hearing these words from a man who owes his
> own spiritual formation from the beginning to Polish
> culture, to its literature, its music, its plastic arts, its
> theatre — to Polish history, to the Polish Christian
> traditions, to the Polish schools, the Polish univer-
> sities. In speaking to you young people in this way,
> this man wishes above all to *pay the debt* that he owes
> this marvelous spiritual heritage that began with the
> Bogurodzica. At the same time, this man wishes to
> appear before you today with this heritage, which
> is the common good of all Poles and constitutes an
> outstanding part of European and world culture.

Those of you who lived through the Communist era will
understand that Communism was its own pseudo-religion.
It was an ideology which offered a materialist anthropology,
a materialist soteriology, and a materialist understanding of
culture. Whereas a Christian culture is partly based on the
belief that the human intellect was made with a capacity to
discern the truth, that the human will was made to pursue
goodness, and that the human memory has a special attraction
to beauty, Communist cultures are characterized by mendacity
rather than truth, cruelty rather than goodness, and ugliness
in every sphere of life rather than beauty. Communism was a
pseudo-religion because it claimed to know the truth about the
human person and to offer a kind of this-worldly salvation as
a member of a class with an historic destiny to eliminate all
social distinctions.

Historians now acknowledge that John Paul II, along with
other significant world-leaders of the 1980s and with the help of
the Polish diaspora, brought about the destruction of European

Communism. One could say that his spiritual capital was of such a magnitude that it inspired a generation to refuse co-operation with the many forms of Communist evil. However, what John Paul II destroyed was a system promoted by what sociologists call "the Old Left" — the hard-core Stalinist types and their quislings. While John Paul II and others were fighting the Old Left in the countries that had been caught on the wrong side of Winston Churchill's "Iron Curtain," the cultures of the countries in the so-called free world were undergoing an anti-Christian revolution fostered by those who described themselves as the "New Left." These types were more interested in gender ideology than the class war, but like the Old Left, their number one enemy was Christianity.

When I was writing my Master's thesis on the Polish anti-Communist intelligentsia in 1989 and living not far from here in Ulica Sienkiewicza, I came across an article by Professor Zdzisław Krasnodębski called "Waiting for Supermarkets." His argument was that the only thing which Western Europe had to offer a post-Communist Poland was supermarkets. Using classical idioms which would be lost on many a Western-educated undergraduate, Krasnodębski wrote: "There is no archaic Ithaca to which we can return because Penelope did not wait faithfully." The point was that even after four decades of Communism, Poland still had more cultural capital at her disposal than the countries of Western Europe, who, having been caught up in the *Zeitgeist* of 1968, had little to offer from their cultural treasuries apart from supermarkets. A similar point was made by the late Václav Havel, in an interview he gave to Adam Michnik, published in 2014. Commenting on what was achieved or maybe not achieved by his "Velvet Revolution" of 1989, Havel remarked:

On the one hand, everything is getting better and better: every week there is a new generation of cell phones. But in order to use one, you need very detailed instructions. And so you read those instructions instead of books and in your free time you watch TV, where a good-looking, tanned young man in a commercial shouts how happy he is that he has swimming trunks from company X. So along with the development of this consumerist global civilization grows a mass of people who do not create any values. They are only intermediaries — public relations agents. . . . All of that seems very dangerous, and I don't know whether civilization on its own will come to its senses without huge quakes or tsunamis. In any case I feel the need for some existential revolution.[2]

If John Paul II had been conducting that interview rather than Adam Michnik, he would probably have replied that Havel's instincts were right — that materialist civilizations, or civilizations that are weak on cultural and spiritual capital, will always be, at best, banal. If one travels to Prague today one finds that the biggest tourist attractions are the library of the Strahov monastery dating from 1143, the Charles Bridge which began to be constructed in 1357, the statue of the Infant King of Prague, which first arrived in Prague in 1556, St Vitus's cathedral which also had its beginnings in medieval times, and some Hapsburg era churches. The Communists produced nothing of beauty and lasting value and post-Communist liberalism has produced numerous tourist shops selling Bohemian glass and refrigerator magnets, and a few good restaurants and hotels.

[2] Elzbieta Matynia (trans.), *An Uncanny Era: Conversations between Václav Havel and Adam Michnik* (Yale University Press, 2014), 153.

Contemporary Western liberalism however has moved beyond a mere marginalization of the spiritual. It is not simply that Christ and indeed the entire Trinity gets forgotten, or taken for granted, because people are more interested in cell phones and swimming trunks. Rather, the ideology of political liberalism which is promoted through the law schools and humanities departments in the great universities of the West is hostile to the whole notion of cultural and spiritual capital. As John Rawls, the designer of political liberalism, expressed the principle, if a man wishes to spend his life counting blades of grass, then that for him is the good life, and no one else has any standing upon which to judge that this particular life-style option is a waste of the gift of time and life. According to the tenets of political liberalism there is no greater form of anti-social behavior than making moral judgments that one life-style choice is superior to another. Underlying this ideology is a rejection of what in classical philosophy were known as the transcendentals: truth, beauty, goodness. As the intellectual historian Charles Taylor has observed, when people reject Christianity, they do not merely reject Christian revelation, they reject everything good in pre-Christian classical culture that found itself baptized by Christianity. This includes the search for truth, the high value given to intellectual life, the quest for personal integrity, and the appreciation of beauty in music, painting, architecture, and human manners.

The predominance of what Pope Benedict called "the dictatorship of relativism" leaves Poland yet again in a position where, if she wishes to retain her independence, she must stand against a powerful ideological tsunami that will not tolerate the existence of a high Christian culture. Poland is like the intellectual boy in the playground who gets bullied because he is smarter than everyone else and knows how to play a violin as well as get his homework 100% correct. The English writer G. K. Chesterton once said:

> I can certainly claim to have been from the first a partisan of the Polish ideal, even when my sympathy was mainly an instinct. (...) It was almost entirely founded on the denunciations of Poland, which were by no means rare. I judged the Poles by their enemies. And I found it was an almost unfailing truth that their enemies were the enemies of magnanimity and man-hood. If a man loved slavery, if he loved usury, if he loved terrorism and all the trampled mire of materi-alistic politics, I have always found that he added to these affections the passion of a hatred of Poland. She could be judged in the light of that hatred; and the judgment has proved to be right.[3]

In different periods in Polish history the attacks come from different directions but always there is the element of hostility to the cultural and spiritual capital of Poland. Karol Wojtyła's belief was that it was precisely this capital which both defines Poland as a nation and is the source of her independence.

Unless national identity rests on something that completely transcends all individuals it will have no power as a social glue. To quote the Scottish philosopher Alasdair MacIntyre, no one wants to die for a telephone company. If nations have no foundations higher than contract law, national identity will be very weak. Instead of a strong nation one has a bureaucratic structure called the government or the state and if its only reason for being is to administer utilities, to keep the telecom-munications system working, and the trains running on time,

[3] Gilbert Keith Chesterton in *Introduction* to *Letters on Polish Affairs*, by Charles Sarolea (Edinburgh: Oliver and Boyd, 1922).

no one will die for that or feel as though a part of one's very identity is molded by it. Similarly, in his work on *Modern Social Imaginaries* Charles Taylor argued that implicit in our social imaginations is the ability to recognize ideal cases and beyond the ideal stands some notion of a moral or metaphysical order, of which the norms and ideals make sense.[4]

Different nations have different foundational narratives, some of which are Christian and some of which are merely deistic, neo-pagan or otherwise anti-Christian. What is happening in the West today is that without a Christian anthropology and soteriology, liberal political theory is fostering a neo-pagan idolatry of the state. As the American theologian William Cavanaugh has expressed the idea, the modern liberal state today has become a parody of the body of Christ. Books are being published with titles like "Worshipping the State: How Liberalism Became Our State Religion." Bureaucrats with their social engineering policies are replacing priests as the chief guardians of moral character. Even children's toys are now the subject of political correctness campaigns and policies. The most recent example was the pressure brought to bear by the United Nations on the company that produces the popular English children's program Thomas the Tank Engine, which I understand appears on Polish Television as *Tomek I Przyjaciele*, to change a number of its male engines to female engines. The engines with the most quintessentially British male names—Henry and Edward—have been axed.

An intellectual history tour explaining how this came about is beyond the scope of this address today. Suffice to say that the Critical Theory of the Frankfurt School of Social Research is an important part of the history. At the Synod on the Family held in Rome in 2015, the President of the Catholic Doctors

---

[4]   Charles Taylor, *Modern Social Imaginaries* (Durham, NC: Duke University Press, 2004), 24.

Society of Bucharest suggested that if Church leaders seriously wanted to understand the collapse of the institution of the family in Western countries they should be holding a Synod on the influence of Frankfurt School philosophy on Catholic theology and political philosophy. I strongly concurred with that assessment.

In his article "Theology and Praxis" published in 1973, Charles Davis, one of the big British Catholic names of the 1960s, and by 1973 a laicized Jesuit, described the attraction of the Frankfurt School's Critical Theory to Belgian and Dutch theologians in the following terms:

> Fundamental for them as a consequence of their acceptance of the Marxist unity of theory and *praxis* is a conviction that the permanent self-identity of the Christian faith cannot be presupposed.... Truth does not yet exist; it cannot be reached by interpretation, but it has to be produced by change. For these theologians therefore, faith is in a strong sense mediated in history through *praxis*. *Praxis* is not the application of already known truth or the carrying out of a transhistorical ideal; it is that process in and through which one comes to know present reality and future possibilities.

Davis goes on to note that if faith is mediated in *praxis*, it must renounce any claim to universality.[5]

In the final paragraph of his article, Davis pointed to the significance of this appropriation of Critical Theory with the rhetorical question: "Is theology, as [Edward] Schillebeeckx says, the critical self-consciousness of Christian *praxis*, or is

---

5 Charles Davis, "Theology and Praxis," *Cross Currents* 2 (1973): 154–68, at 167.

[Leszek] Kołakowski right when he says: 'For theology begins with the belief that truth has already been given to us, and its intellectual effort consists not of attrition against reality but of assimilation of something which is ready in its entirety'?"[6]

In my judgement Kołakowski was right and Schillebeeckx was wrong. Today I would argue that there are more people at Mass in Poland each day than there are in Germany because Polish clerical leaders have consistently followed the position Davis associated with Kołakowski, while German clerical leaders, with some notable exceptions, for example Ratzinger and Meisner, have tended to follow Schillebeeckx.

To put the issue more simply, is faith something we receive as a gift, or is it something we construct for ourselves? The idea that faith is a gift received to be faithfully transmitted from generation to generation lies at the heart of the cultural capital of Poland, and thus Polish independence, as Karol Wojtyła understood it.

For the faith to be successfully transmitted we need saints. In addition to the poets and philosophers, the musicians, and other artists, for a nation to have a strong and non-banal culture, it needs saints. St John Paul II went about canonizing a large number of saints because he understood their importance for the cultural memory of a nation. As the Swiss theologian Hans Urs von Balthasar noted:

> Those who withdraw to the heights to fast and pray in silence are . . . the pillars bearing the spiritual weight of what happens in history. They share in the unique-ness of Christ, in the freedom of that nobility which is conferred from above; that serene, untamed freedom which cannot be caged and put to use. Theirs is the

[6]   Ibid.

first of all aristocracies, source and justification for all the others, and the last yet remaining to us in a most unaristocratic age.[7]

Not only did the scholars and artists of the period of the partitions protect and develop the cultural capital of Poland, but alongside them there were Polish saints bearing the lion's share of the spiritual weight. Some of the important names in this context were: Bogdan Jański, Edmund Bojanowski, Raphael Kalinowski, Albert Chmielowski, Urszula Ledóchowska, August Czartoryski, Wanda Malczewska, Bronisław Markiewicz, and Honorat Kozminski. Chmielowski, who was one of those saints canonized by St. John Paul II, could be said to have contributed to Polish independence on *every* front — the military, the intellectual, the artistic, and above all the spiritual. Similarly, Urszula Ledóchowska was a great advocate for Polish independence, a subject she often addressed while speaking at conferences across Scandinavia at a time when she was opening convents in Russia, while Honorat Kozminski went about defying Russian orders by setting up new religious communities in those parts of Poland partitioned by Russia.

Many other examples could be given of the contributions to Polish independence made through the defense and development of the spiritual and cultural capital of Poland. The spiritual and cultural capital, are of course, inter-dependent on each other. They are not two separate things, but two connected things, like the divinity and humanity of Christ.

I will conclude with Wojtyła's poem, "Thinking My Country":

Freedom — a continuing conquest,
It cannot simply be possessed!

[7] Hans Urs von Balthasar, *A Theology of History* (London: Sheed & Ward, 1963), 125.

It comes as a gift, but keeping it is a struggle.
Gift and struggle are inscribed on pages, hidden yet
  open.
For freedom you pay with all your being, therefore
  call that your freedom
Which allows you, in paying the price,
To possess yourself ever anew.
At such a price do we enter history and touch her
  epochs.
Where is the dividing-line between those generations
  who paid too little
And those who paid too much?
On which side of that line are we?[8]

---

[8] Karol Wojtyła, *Collected Poems*, trans. Jerzy Pietrkiewicz (New York: Random House, 1982).

9

Tea with Honey,
But Not in Jerusalem

D R ROWAN WILLIAMS IS RETIRING AS the Archbishop of Canterbury to take up the post of Master of Magdalene College, Cambridge. His "valedictory" book, *Faith in the Public Square*, is attracting considerable media interest. In a colorful review in the *London Catholic Herald*, Dr William Oddie concluded that the ideas promoted in the book are the sort of impractical nonsense one only hears on Oxbridge high tables and in senior common rooms.

The macro-level point of the book was that it is possible to distinguish between what Dr Williams calls "procedural secularism" and "programmatic secularism." He offers the practices of the Indian government as an example of "procedural secularism," and of the French as an example of "programmatic secularism." He could equally have placed Australia in the "procedural secularism" category.

The hallmark of "procedural secularism" is that governments do not privilege any one faith. For example, in Australia all religious schools receive some government funding. It doesn't matter whether the "religion" is Islam, Judaism, or some form of Christianity. No one faith community gets a better funding deal than any other. Dr Williams is in favor of this kind of "procedural secularism."

However he opposes "programmatic secularism" which bans all faiths from the public realm. He also notes that "secularism in its neat distillation is inseparable from functionalism" and that "in having no criteria other than functional ones,

Published in Crisis Magazine, *October 2, 2012.*

secularism takes for granted contests of power as the basic form of social relations." He doesn't like this latent social Darwinism and he is well aware that "secularism fails to sustain the imaginative life." He argues that "religious convictions should be granted a public hearing in debate, but not necessarily one in which they are privileged or regarded as being beyond criticism." So-called "public reason" should be a sufficiently broad concept to encompass religious convictions. Governments, he suggests, should see themselves as a community of communities rather than as a monopolistic sovereign power.

When it comes to human rights, Dr Williams acknowledges that Alasdair MacIntyre has a strong point in his criticism of the liberal tradition of rights, including his provocative assertion that such "rights" have no more basis in reality than a belief in witches and unicorns. However, Williams wants to push on with the use of "rights" language at the same time as presenting programmatic secularists with something like the MacIntyrean critique of the liberal natural right tradition. Williams concludes that "the uncomfortable truth is that a purely secularist account of human rights is always going to be problematic if it attempts to establish a language of rights as a supreme and non-contestable governing concept in ethics." In short, without something like the *Imago Dei* underpinning the rights jurisprudence, not only do rights have no foundation apart from power politics, but we have no criteria for determining what is or is not a "right" other than by reference to power politics. A right becomes whatever you have the power to assert.

In drawing distinctions between different types of secularism as he does, Williams's proposals are evocative of the "perfectionist liberalism" of Joseph Raz and the theory of "communicative action" of Jürgen Habermas. There is a heavy emphasis on the "Anglican virtues" of compromise, middle paths, dialogue and debate. What one doesn't find is a grand soteriological vision, a passionate enunciation of what the United Kingdom could be with reference to elements in the Christian faith. There is no defense of the United Kingdom as a Christian kingdom. Christians are told not to be concerned about their fate in what is rapidly becoming a post-Christian culture, because that is "in God's hands."

In the final analysis, notwithstanding the many very reasonable observations made about how to conduct a dialogue with people from other faiths and none, Oddie has a point. What was missing in the work was an engagement with the problem of evil. It is a sociological fact that not every member of the community is into Oxbridge common room urbanity, and anyone who has been anywhere near an Oxbridge College knows that behind all the urbanity there is no politics as lethal as academic politics. The battles are simply fought in a different forum.

Until the end of the world there will be what Hans Urs von Balthasar called the "battle of the Logos." Members of the city of God will be persecuted by members of the city of man. Christians are not only up against militant materialists but they have to contend with the powers and principalities of the "Prince of this World." As St. Paul noted: "Our wrestling is not against flesh and blood; but against principalities and powers, against the rulers of the world of this darkness, against the spirits of wickedness in the high places."

Tolkien and C. S. Lewis had a deep understanding of this state of play. The battles are different for each generation, but there are always battles.

The British national myth or "social imagery" in whatever manifestation, from Shakespeare's sceptered isle with its kings renowned for their "Christian service and true chivalry" to C. S. Lewis's *Chronicles of Narnia*, rests on the notion that the British lion, call him Aslan or Alfred, Richard or George, is a Christian lion. No doubt this Christian lion has good Oxbridge virtues, like urbanity, civility, respect for other people because they are God's creatures too, regardless of what theological nonsense they might believe, but he is also a lion who has to roar and fight. He has taken on all manner of psychopaths from Napoleon to Bismarck to Hitler.

The negative reviews of *Faith in the Public Square* seem to arise from the impression that Dr Williams wants the fruits of a Christian culture while being somewhat shy about the idea that we might actually have to fight for these fruits. He wants the civility of Rupert Brooke's honey with tea served under the cherry trees in Grantchester meadow, but he doesn't quite have a strategy for engaging with Sauron and Morgoth apart from inviting them to tea. Those who do, like members of the British SAS sleeping in snake ridden caves in Afghanistan, need to believe that they are risking their lives for something a little more eternal than mere "argumentative democracy."

If I were a UK soldier in Afghanistan I would be there serving Her Majesty, Queen Elizabeth II. I would have taken an oath of loyalty to her. She in turn took her Coronation Oath on the Gospels. She believes that she serves the Christian God. The chapel in her castle is named in honor of St. George. He is represented on the Union Jack by the red stripes. The blue and white stripes are in honor of St. Andrew — another Christian martyr.

Dr Williams is critical of consumerism and the idea that our human relationships should be defined by market forces, and he acknowledges that secularism fails to sustain the imaginative life, but what exactly is the alternative if singing *Jerusalem* becomes politically incorrect or even banned as hate speech?

The imaginations of British youth need to be nourished on something. I agree with Dr Williams that I wouldn't offer them Adam Smith's *The Wealth of Nations* as a first choice — but what's wrong with fighting *for* the legitimacy of Aslan's New Jerusalem?

10

A Pope Who Thinks in Centuries

I N 1963 COLUMBIA PICTURES PRODUCED
the movie *The Cardinal*. According to Wikipedia, the Vatican's liaison officer on the project was a young Joseph
Ratzinger. In the movie there is a dialogue between a couple
of venerable curial officials and a young monsignor. The monsignor explains that if the Vatican could just be a little more
flexible on some of its political policies, the social standing
of Catholics in the United States could dramatically improve
within a decade. The officials exchange "he has so much to
learn" looks and reply, "The Church, Msgr. Fermoyle, thinks
in centuries, not decades."

This is a point no one would ever have needed to make to the
young Benedict. One might say that he was born with a nose for
history. Many of his early publications were in the territory of
the theology of history, soteriology, and eschatology, and even
his ecclesiology was framed within these horizons. His vision
of the Church is that of a divine institution with a particular
mission in history against which the gates of hell cannot prevail.

At least one effect of this vision is that he is less concerned
than many others of his generation about popularity polls
and political correctness. It is a very brave world leader who
dares to suggest that there might be some issues about the
relationship between faith and reason that the Islamic tradition
rather urgently needs to address. The fact that in his Regensburg
speech he also suggested that the will of the individual is no
more reliable a standard than the will of Allah, and thus that
Western liberalism also needs to think more deeply about the
faith and reason relationship, went largely unreported, except

Published in the Catholic World Report, *April 18, 2010.*

by Professor Schall from Georgetown. One gets the impression that Benedict's analyses are often too nuanced for the average journalist to digest.

One solution might be for his press office to produce "background briefing" papers for journalists with short historical memories. For example, it is hard to make sense of his going out on a limb to release the Lefebrvist bishops from the penalty of excommunication unless one understands how deep is the rift within the Church in France, what happened to French Catholics during the Revolution, and how foolish it was for 1960s-generation ecclesial leaders to present documents like *Dignitatis Humanae* to the French as the Church's endorsement of the French Revolution. The 1960s generation was at best indifferent and often quite hostile to history and tradition. This was bad anthropology. Benedict now has to contend with the pastoral mess this "bull in a china shop" behavior created.

Without such an appreciation of the historical background, the Pope's extraordinary efforts to bring back wounded and disgruntled sheep could look like what Hans Küng called "fishing in the muddy waters of right-wing extremists," but it is not. It's his job to go after the lost sheep and care for them individually, rather than treating them as mere "collateral damage" in the forward march of history toward a more modernity-friendly world-ethos, as Küng would have it.

On the positive side of the ledger his speeches and homilies have been inspirational. Often busy leaders rely on the speeches they are handed by aides which were drafted by committees with all the compromises this inevitably entails. However, when Benedict speaks one senses that he has written the material himself, and it is never bland. His Wednesday audience addresses, or "Catechetics 101 classes," have been immensely popular. Catholics have enjoyed the weekly installments on the adventures of the Apostles and the contributions of the early Church Fathers. They have also taken up reading *Jesus of Nazareth*, a book that has been popular with Christians from all denominations.

Indeed, those in the Wednesday audience crowds include many Christians who are not Catholic. Unlike a lot of Italian and Spanish ecclesial leaders who spend their entire childhoods never meeting a Protestant, Benedict comes from the country where Protestantism began. His homilies are also Christocentric and scriptural and this is music to the ears of many Protestants. He speaks a theological dialect they understand.

Relations with the Orthodox have also improved. Archbishop Alfeyev of the Moscow Patriarchate has even established the St. Gregory Nazianzen Foundation to form a European Catholic-Orthodox Alliance against "secularism, liberalism, and relativism." Like members of the Traditional Anglican Communion, the Orthodox consider magisterial teachings against the ordination of women and homosexual marriage to be reasons for respecting the Petrine Office and establishing closer relations with it.

The traditional Anglicans are not Protestants in the usual sense. Most often they are people who have been deterred from swimming the Tiber by their knowledge of what Digby Anderson calls "the oikish translation of the Mass" that awaits them on the other side, or because they are not comfortable rubbing shoulders in the pews with Fenian sympathizers. Benedict has been sensitive to these cultural factors. While the Fenian issue is really outside of his jurisdiction, he has at least allowed the Anglicans to keep their own rite of the Mass at the same time as he proceeds with the reform of the Roman rite, in particular the reform of those "oikish translations."

In general, one might summarize the first five years by saying that this papacy has been focused on healing the schisms of the 11th and 16th centuries and the problems created by the application of the "hermeneutic of rupture" to the documents of the Second Vatican Council, including the schism of 1988. It has been a papacy devoted to Christian unity. This has required a certain sensitivity to historical and theological differences not often possessed by the average secular journalist. Someone with Benedict's intellectual ability and "nose for history" is very well placed to do this and he has bravely taken the flak, especially from people who either can't think beyond the present or want it to be forever 1968.

The Communist Party of the Soviet Union thought in terms of five-year plans, not centuries, and today it is out of business. Meanwhile *Pravda* carries an editorial in praise of a pope who dares to think beyond the next five years.

11

The New Pontifical Academy
for Latin

POPE BENEDICT HAS ANNOUNCED THE creation of a new Pontifical Academy for Latin, which will be linked to the work of the Pontifical Council for Culture. It's a good moment to do so.

The study of Latin has been in the doldrums ever since Catholics parted with "the speech of Christian centuries" and became "like profane intruders in the literary precincts of sacred utterance" (to quote from the General Audience Address of Paul VI on November 26, 1969).

In the 1960s the study of Latin went out at about the same pace as the practice of wearing hats and gloves to Mass. In my school in provincial Australia, the subject was entirely dropped from the curriculum and replaced by the more commercially-oriented Japanese. Our local economy ran on coal and beef (which was exported to Japan) and the Iwasaki Resort, a holiday destination for wealthy (predominantly Japanese) golfers.

Not only in provincial Australia, but in the world at large, "relevance" was then a buzzword, and being relevant meant being economically competitive or otherwise able to improve one's standard of living. While there is nothing wrong with wanting to improve one's standard of living, it does become a problem if this objective is treated as a highest good to which all else is subordinated.

The practice of correlating education to the acquisition of market-driven "skills" has led to a general impoverishment of the cultural capital of the entire Western world. This is

Published in The Catholic Thing, November 15, 2012.

a particular problem for the Church because philistinism is toxic to what Pope Benedict calls "the humanism of the Incarnation."

One notable exception who held out against the rising tide of philistinism was the Discalced Carmelite Fr. Reginald ("Reggie") Foster. Originally from the archdiocese of Milwaukee, he began to teach Latin at the Gregorian University in the 1970s. Fr. Foster formerly worked for the "Latin Letters" section of the Secretariat of State in the Vatican, which was once responsible for sending briefs to princes.

In 1985, Fr. Foster began offering a series of Summer Latin intensives known as the *Aestiva Romae Latinitas*. Students from all over the world attended these classes. He eventually found himself in some trouble with the accountants at the Gregorian for not charging his poorer students. Nonetheless, he managed to form another couple of generations of Latin scholars who can take up his work at the newly created Pontifical Academy.

Fr. Foster was fond of reading the sermons of St. Leo of the Great in Latin and so it was highly appropriate that Pope Benedict's *Motu Proprio* "Lingua Latina," establishing the Academy, was promulgated on the Feast of St. Leo the Great.

The aims of the Academy are: (a) to promote the knowledge and study of the Latin language and literature in its classical, patristic, medieval, and humanistic forms, especially in Catholic educational institutions in which both seminarians and priests are formed and instructed; and (b) to promote in different spheres the use of Latin both as a written and spoken language.

The creation of the Academy represents an endorsement of Pope John XXIII's 1962 Apostolic Constitution *Veterum Sapientia*. John XXIII endorsed the use of Latin not merely as a passport to a proper understanding of Christian writers of antiquity, or from a desire for bureaucratic uniformity, but as an element of the Church's tradition that is valuable for "religious reasons." He argued that the Church, precisely because she embraces all nations and is destined to endure until the end of time, by her very nature requires a language that is universal, immutable, and non-vernacular. The use of a dead language privileges no particular national group but unites all in a common linguistic tradition. John XXIII claimed, moreover, that it is altogether fitting that the language of the Church should be noble and majestic and non-vernacular since the Church has a dignity far surpassing that of every merely human society.

In his book on the history of Poland, *God's Playground*, Norman Davies quotes Daniel Defoe (the author of *Robinson Crusoe*) to the effect that, in the eighteenth century, a traveler could easily move across the length and breadth of Poland without any knowledge of the Polish language. All one needed was Latin.

Latin (along with classical Greek and Hebrew) provides a kind of linguistic glue for the intellectual heritage of the West. If the Church wants to nourish scholarship and be the guardian of the great cultural treasures of the Christian centuries, then she needs to foster the study of the classical languages. Pope Benedict is acutely aware of this. When he was a Cardinal, Pope Benedict argued that seminaries need to be places of broad cultural formation. He conceded that it wasn't possible to do everything, but he argued that seminary professors should not "surrender to philistinism."

We have a pope who speaks five modern languages and is quite at home with Classical Greek, Latin, and Hebrew. He plays the piano and is a member of the *Académie française*, arguably the most prestigious academic club in the world. His creation of a Pontifical Academy for Latin is a significant initiative in the battle against what Alexander Boot in *How the West Was Lost* has called "Modman Philistine's" attempted destruction of the high culture of the Western world. That culture is rooted in the literature of the cities of Rome, Athens, and Jerusalem — and, of course, in the event of the Incarnation, the center and purpose of all human history.

12

Benedict XVI and the
End of the Virtual Council

I N ONE OF THE LAST ACTS OF HIS PONTIF-
icate, Benedict XVI gave an address to the clergy of the
Diocese of Rome on the Second Vatican Council.[1] In the
address he drew a distinction between what he termed the
Virtual Council, or Council of the Media, and the Real Council
or Council of those who actually produced the documents. He
observed that since the Council of the Media was accessible
to everyone (not just to students of theology who studied the
documents), it became the dominant interpretation and this
created "many disasters" and "much suffering." Specifically,
he mentioned the closure of seminaries and convents, and
the promotion of banal liturgy, and the application of notions
of popular sovereignty to issues of Church governance. He
concluded however that some 50 years after the Council, "this
virtual Council is broken, is lost."

From what comes across my desk, there is still a lot of life in
the Virtual Council, though it is true that it holds no enchant-
ment for young seminarians or members of new ecclesial movements and thus the Church of the future will, as a matter of
demography, be more closely oriented by the documents of
the Real Council.

When John Paul II lay dying he said to the youth who had
travelled to Rome to offer their prayerful support: "I have
searched for you, and now you have come to me, and I thank

[1] Benedict XVI, Meeting with Parish Priests and the Clergy of Rome,
Paul VI Audience Hall, Vatican City, February 14, 2013.

Published in the Catholic World Report, *April 19, 2013.*

you." Less irenically he might have said, "I have tried to get through to you, notwithstanding layers and layers of deaf and dumb bureaucrats, and now that I am dying, the fact that you are here means that at least some of you understood, and this is my consolation." Similarly, Benedict seemed to be saying to the clergy of Rome, notwithstanding all the banality, all the pathetic liturgies, all the congregationalist ecclesiology, the Virtual Council of the Media has lost its dynamism. It is no longer potent. It no longer sets the course of human lives, it no longer inspires rebellion. It, too, has become boring and sterile.

In this particular address, Benedict divided the documents of the Council into two broad categories: first, there were the documents inspired by what he called the "Rhineland alliance" — the network of young theologians from France, Germany, Belgium, Holland, and Austria. These were the documents on the liturgy (*Sacrosanctum Concilium*), on the Church (*Lumen Gentium*), on Scripture, Tradition and Revelation (*Dei Verbum*) and on ecumenism (*Unitatis Redintegratio*). In some ways these documents were mopping up the unfinished business of the First Vatican Council, which was brought to an untimely end by the Franco-Prussian war. Certainly, the theology which underpinned these documents had been developing in the decades between the two World Wars and did not suddenly crop up at the Council.

While the members of the Rhineland alliance were interested in ecclesiology and liturgical theology, ecumenism and scriptural exegesis, the Americans wanted a declaration on religious liberty to deal with their politico-theological problems, the French were similarly concerned with the whole complex phenomenon of modernity, and yet others, deeply horrified by what had happened to the Jewish people in ostensibly Christian countries, saw the need for some statement about the covenant of the Old Testament and Judaism in general. As a consequence the documents *Dignitatis Humanae, Nostra Aetate,* and *Gaudium et Spes* became a second "very important trilogy." Of all these documents the two closest to the heart of Ratzinger were *Dei Verbum,* the Dogmatic Constitution on Divine Revelation and *Lumen Gentium,* the Dogmatic Constitution on the Church. As a young conciliar *peritus* (expert theological advisor) Professor Ratzinger was involved in the drafting of *Dei Verbum* and his patron Cardinal Frings also intervened extensively in the debate on this document. Ratzinger's reflections on these interventions were published in an article in the journal *Communio* in 1988. In this article he recalled Cardinal Frings's argument that when one speaks of the two sources of revelation as scripture and tradition, one is right at the level of epistemology; we do experience what revelation is from scripture and from tradition. Nonetheless Frings also argued that the "scripture and tradition, two sources formula" was false if looked at from a metaphysical perspective, since both scripture and tradition flow from revelation as their common source. The problem with the epistemological focus is that "if one does not hold that revelation precedes its objectification in scripture and tradition, remaining always greater than they, then the concept of revelation is reduced to the dimensions of the historical and simply human."[2]

In *Dei Verbum* the Fathers of the Council overcame various theological problems by holding that Christ himself is the revelation of God the Father to humanity and that both scripture and tradition flow from this revelation. *Dei Verbum* is thus a classic example of how the Council reformed an area

---

[2] Joseph Ratzinger, "Cardinal Frings's Speeches During the Second Vatican Council: Apropos of A. Muggeridge's *The Desolate City," Communio: International Catholic Review* Vol 15(1) (Spring 1988): 131–47; republished in *Joseph Ratzinger in Communio,* Vol 1, *The Unity of the Church* (Grand Rapids: Eerdmans, 2010), 93.

of theology which had given rise to a rather large number of problems from at least as far back as the 16th century.

In particular, in an article published in 1969 in Herbert Vorgrimler's *Commentaries on the Documents of the Council,* Ratzinger stated that in the drafting of *Dei Verbum* the conciliar fathers were "concerned with overcoming neo-scholastic intellectualism, for which revelation chiefly meant a store of mysterious supernatural teachings, which automatically reduces faith very much to an acceptance of these supernatural insights."[3] This was the archetypically Suárezian account of revelation, which contemporary historical scholarship (see for example, the work of John Montag[4]) now regards as a reversal of the position of classical Thomism. For Suárez, revelation did not disclose God himself, but rather pieces of information about God. When Ratzinger was a student the Suárezian account was dominant, to such a degree that when he criticized it in his *Habilitation* thesis, preferring the position of St. Bonaventure, he was forced to withdraw the criticism or suffer the penalty of not passing the thesis. At Vatican II however, the Council Fathers were persuaded of the merits of the approach advanced by Cardinal Frings, which had no doubt been influenced by the ideas of the young Professor Ratzinger.

While *Dei Verbum* addressed the topics of scripture, tradition, and revelation, *Lumen Gentium* focused on ecclesiology. The "reform" engendered here was one of moving away from a primarily juridical account of the Church focused on the distinction between clerical and lay members to an understanding based on multidimensional relationships.

[3] Joseph Ratzinger, "Dogmatic Constitution on Divine Revelation: Origin and Background," in Herbert Vorgrimler, *Commentary on the Documents of Vatican II,* Vol. III (New York: Herder and Herder, 1969), 172.

[4] John Montag, "The False Legacy of Suárez," in John Milbank, Catherine Pickstock, and Graham Ward (eds), *Radical Orthodoxy* (London: Routledge, 1999), 38–64.

With reference to the notion of sacramental relations, Henri de Lubac emphasized that the sacramental form of relationality is one that ties together the Church as the mystical body of Christ with the Church as the historical people of God. Moreover, the Church not only links the visible with the invisible, time with eternity, but also the universal and the particular, the Old and New Covenants. This link between the invisible and visible elements of ecclesial communion constitutes the Church as the Sacrament of salvation. Thus, in chapter 1 of *Lumen Gentium* one finds the following declaration:

> Christ, the one mediator, set up his holy Church here on earth as a visible structure, a community of faith, hope and love; and he sustains it unceasingly and through it he pours out grace and truth on everyone. This society, however, equipped with hierarchical structures, and the mystical body of Christ, a visible assembly and a spiritual community, an earthly church and a church enriched with heavenly gifts, must not be considered as two things, but as forming a complex reality comprising a human and divine element. It is therefore by no mean analogy that it is likened to the mystery of the Incarnate Word.

Concomitant with this move away from a focus on a juridical notion of the Church with its primary distinction between priestly and other religious members on the one side, and lay members on the other, was the Council's endorsement of a universal call to holiness.

Notwithstanding this affirmation of a variety of spiritual missions in the life of the Church, some lay and some clerical, *Lumen Gentium* nonetheless affirmed the authority of the Petrine Office and the sacerdotal priesthood. There was nothing in this document that could in any way justify the subsequent attacks on the papacy and the priesthood which were some of the more infamous products of the Virtual Council in the decade of the 1970s and beyond.

In 1972 Joseph Ratzinger, along with Hans Urs von Balthasar and Henri de Lubac, founded the theology journal which they named *Communio*. It would be too simplistic to describe it as a response to the Virtual Council because, in addition to the Virtual Council there was also the Council of other conciliar *periti* who, as the decade of the 1970s wore on, closely associated themselves with the rival journal *Concilium*. The English historian Philip Trower has described the intellectual battle between the two different interpretations of the Council as presented in the pages of *Communio* and *Concilium* as "a theological star wars" played out over the heads of the faithful. In other words, what people in parishes received as the "teaching of the Council" was often the residue of ideas floated by the former *periti* in one or other of these journals. Since the *Concilium* interpretations were often a lot closer to the interpretations of the Virtual Council, during the final years of the pontificate of Paul VI they tended to dominate.

However, in 1985 John Paul II called a Synod to reflect on the various interpretations of the Council, and following this Synod the *Communio* ecclesiology began to receive strong magisterial endorsement. Pope Benedict obliquely referred to this in his address to the clergy of Rome. Speaking of the concept of communion, he remarked that although, philologically speaking, it was not fully developed at the Council, it was nonetheless as a result of the Council that "the concept of communion came more and more to be the expression of the Church's essence, communion in its different dimensions: communion with the Trinitarian God — who is himself communion between Father, Son and Holy Spirit — sacramental communion, and concrete communion in the episcopate and in the life of the Church." In this address he added that the application of the *Communio* ecclesiology to the life of the Church is "not yet complete" and that "more needs to be done."

The conciliar document which was least acceptable to Ratzinger was *Gaudium et Spes*. Along with Cardinal Walter Kasper and others he argued that a major problem with this document is that it was poorly drafted. In particular the first sections were not well integrated with the later sections. The anthropology of the first section has been described as "merely theistically colored," whereas the anthropology of later sections is explicitly Trinitarian. It is well known that John Paul II was deeply influenced by paragraph 22 of this document and that this particular paragraph looks as though it was lifted almost word for word from an earlier work by Henri de Lubac. Paragraph 22 is explicitly Christocentric. Ratzinger also strongly approved of Paragraph 22 and described the document as a whole as offering a "daring new" theological anthropology which he endorsed, although he thought it had not been well articulated.

As a consequence of the drafting issues and of the under-developed theology in some areas, *Gaudium et Spes* tended to give rise to two different interpretations of the relationship of the Church to the world and two different pastoral strategies. In short-hand terms they could be described as the Christo-centric Trinitarianism of John Paul II and Benedict, and the correlationism of theologians such as Edward Schillebeeckx. Both care about the "world" and regard it as the theatre of salvation. Neither favors a retreat to the ghetto. One however looks for points of convergence between the faith and contem-porary fashionable philosophies, the other is sacramental in its orientation and seeks to transform the world, to "restore all things in Christ." Another way to put this is to say that the correlationist strategy tends to separate "Christian values" from

"Christian sacraments" and to find points of agreement between the so-called "Christian values" (distilled from actual belief in Christ and participation in the sacramental life of the Church) and non-Christian values. The most common example of this is the promotion of Christian philanthropic projects. The idea is that the "sacramental stuff" is a private matter for private consumption while working for social justice is a public enterprise. Today it is becoming increasingly common for Catholics who find themselves in debates with atheists to refer to the philanthropic works of the Church as a justification for the Catholic faith. Atheists typically respond with indignation because it is quite clear to them that it is possible to have philanthropy without being burdened by Christian morality.

Ratzinger took the atheists' point in an article he published in 1969 on the subject of human dignity in *Gaudium et Spes*. He suggested that according to one reading of *Gaudium et Spes* (one might call it the Virtual Council reading, though he didn't use that expression in 1969), there *is no reason* why the average person of good will should suddenly be burdened with the story of Christ. In other words, some readings of *Gaudium et Spes* beg the question: Does the Incarnation actually make *any* difference?

If one zeroes in on paragraph 22 and treats it as the hermeneutical lens through which the remainder of the document is studied, one sees that the Incarnation is absolutely central and not something that can be distilled out of the account.

In his Trinitarian encyclicals (*Redemptor Hominis, Dives in Misericordia,* and *Dominum et Vivificantem*) John Paul II followed through the logic of this paragraph with the development of a theological anthropology which became one of the most significant theological achievements of his pontificate. Ratzinger was completely behind this project.

In his own pontificate, however, Benedict focused more on the problem of Virtual Council interpretations of *Sacrosanctum*

Concilium than on secularist renderings of *Gaudium et Spes* (which John Paul II had gone a long way towards resolving, at least at the intellectual level). In his books *A New Song for the Lord, Feast of Faith,* and *The Spirit of the Liturgy,* and in his Apostolic Exhortation *Sacramentum Caritatis,* Ratzinger/Benedict offered a remedial liturgical theology.

In his address to the clergy of Rome he also offered the following summary of the Virtual Council's approach to the liturgy:

> There was no interest in liturgy as an act of faith, but as something where comprehensible things are done, a matter of community activity, something profane. And we know that there was a tendency, not without a certain historical basis, to say: sacrality is a pagan thing, perhaps also a thing of the Old Testament. In the New Testament it matters only that Christ died *outside*: that is, outside the gates, in the profane world. Sacrality must therefore be abolished, and profaneness now spreads to worship: worship is no longer worship, but a community act, with communal participation: participation understood as activity. These translations, trivializations of the idea of the Council, were virulent in the process of putting the liturgical reform into practice; they were born from a vision of the Council detached from its proper key, that of faith.

If one combs through the many homilies and articles and books written by Ratzinger/Benedict for comments on the Council, the consistent thread running through everything is that the conciliar documents need to be read with a Christocentric Trinitarian accent.

The central message of *Dei Verbum* is that Christ is the revelation of the Father to humanity; the central message of

Gaudium et Spes is that the Incarnation explains what it means to be human; the central message of *Sacrosanctum Concilium* is that worship is about an encounter with God, a participation in the life of the Trinity, not mere duty parade; and the *Communio* theology implicit in *Lumen Gentium* is thoroughly Trinitarian. When it comes to the relationship between the Old Testament and the New, it is Christ who is the bridge. Even "the sacred mystery of the unity of the Church … finds its highest exemplar and source in the unity of the Persons of the Trinity: the Father and the Son in the Holy Spirit, one God."

There is nothing at all in this Trinitarian hermeneutic about Vatican II being a romance between the Holy Spirit and the *Zeitgeist* of the 1960s.

13

The Ratzinger Revolution

POPE BENEDICT WILL CELEBRATE HIS 90th birthday on Easter Sunday. Cardinal Meisner famously described him as a man who is as intelligent as twelve professors and as pious as a child making his First Communion.

If one inserts the words "Joseph Ratzinger" into the Google Scholar search engine which records academic publications (not tweets and blogs) one obtains some 24,600 hits in four seconds. The word "Benedict XVI" brings up even more results — some 66,100. As a comparison Walter Kasper scores a mere 6,930 and Hans Küng 6,270. Hans Urs von Balthasar and Henri de Lubac score 16,900 and 13,200 hits respectively. The only theologian of the last century I could find who trumps the 66,100 figure is Karl Barth who has been the subject of a massive 127,000 academic articles. The Catholic theologian who came closest to Ratzinger was Karl Rahner weighing in at 41,500 hits.

As Bavaria's most famous son since Ludwig II enters his tenth decade of life it is worth considering what the impact of all these publications might be in the brave new world of 21st-century Catholicism.

My thought is that the publications of Ratzinger will form a treasury to be mined by future generations trying to piece together elements of a fragmented Christian culture.

Ratzinger himself emphasizes that the seat of all faith is the *memoria Ecclesiae*, the memory of the Church. He believes that "there can be a waxing or waning, a forgetting or remembering, but no recasting of truth in time." As a consequence, "the decisive question for today is whether that memory, through

---

Published in the London Catholic Herald, *April 13, 2017.*

which the Church becomes Christ and without which she sinks into nothingness, can continue to exist."

In this void of nothingness, in a world without the *memoria Ecclesiae*, the human person strives for an autonomy that is in conflict with his nature. It is natural, normal, and healthy for one's sense of self to exist within the context of a living history and tradition. Those without such moorings often spend their entire youth trying to "find themselves" without much success and often only after years of painful experimentation.

These reflections on the importance of memory were made by Ratzinger in 1982. Earlier in 1958 during his theological teenager phase, a 31-year-old Ratzinger wrote an essay entitled "The New Pagans and the Church." In this he observed that whenever people make a new acquaintance they can assume with some certainly that the person has a baptismal certificate, but not that he has a Christian frame of mind. This was a full decade before the cultural revolution of the 1960s.

Today we cannot even presume the existence of the baptismal certificate. Members of the millennial generation find themselves in a situation where they have rarely experienced a fully functional Christian social milieu. To find out about Christianity, especially the Catholic version of it, they watch documentaries and movies, they interrogate older Catholics, they Google information about the saints, liturgies, and cultural practices. The cultural capital that should follow as a natural endowment upon their baptism has been frittered away, buried, and in some cases even suppressed, by previous generations. They are like archeologists. They discover fragments of the faith which they find attractive and then they try and work out where the fragment once fitted into a Catholic mental universe.

When a new generation arises in full rebellion from the social experiments of the contemporary era, craving a human ecology that respects both God and nature, and wanting to be something more than rootless cosmopolitans, Ratzinger's publications will serve as the "port-keys" giving creative young rebels access to the missing cultural capital—indeed, access to what Ratzinger calls the *memoria Ecclesiae*.

High on the list of the missing cultural capital is the understanding that, from the earliest times, Christianity has understood itself as the religion of the "Logos," as the religion according to reason. As Ratzinger expresses the principle: "Faith has the right to be missionary only if it transcends all [human] traditions and constitutes an appeal to reason and an orientation toward the truth itself." The lack of truth, he argues, is the major disease our age.

One of Ratzinger's own mentors was Romano Guardini. Guardini wrote that "the Church forgives everything more readily than an attack on truth. She [the Church] knows that if a man falls, but leaves truth unimpaired, he will find his way back again. But if he attacks the vital principle, then the sacred order of life is demolished." In particular Guardini argued that the human will "has to admit that it is blind and needs the light, the leadership, and the organizing formative power of truth. It must admit as a fundamental principle the primacy of knowledge over the will, of the logos over the ethos." Being well intentioned is necessary but not sufficient. Cardinal Pell famously described the idea that it doesn't matter if we make poor judgments providing we mean well as the Donald Duck heresy. Donald is always making mistakes but he rarely intends any harm. Using an expression from Albert Görres, Ratzinger has argued that the mentality that wants to prioritize ethos over logos represents the "Hinduisation" of the faith.

Conversely, and with equal vigor, Ratzinger has emphasized that knowing the content of the faith, having an expert knowledge of all the doctrines, is not sufficient, unless the heart is opened by grace. The human intellect needs to search for the truth. It was made for this. In like manner, the human will was made for goodness, and unless the will is attracted to the good, the intellect is likely to go astray. This is what Ratzinger means when he uses the medieval maxim "reason has a wax nose." As most barristers know, the human intellect can be used to formulate arguments to defend all kinds of actions and propositions.

The human head and the human heart thus need to work in tandem. Both require a Christian formation. In this context Ratzinger often asserts that "love and reason are the twin pillars of all reality."

Without these twin pillars in full operational order, people end up as "narrative wrecks." Without the truth some people are morally rudderless and engage in all manner of self-harming behavior. There is no rationality giving unity to their actions. Others have the truth, but since they do not love, their human formation is stunted and they often cause great harm to other people.

To those who experiment with all manner of psychotherapy, drugs, and Eastern mystical religions in order to discover their inner self, Ratzinger offers the advice that the human person can only find his center of gravity from a position outside of his self. It is Christ who is the center of gravity of every human life. It is Christ who holds a vision not merely of a perfected humanity understood as a universal concept, but for each individual person He holds a vision of what that unique person could be in co-operation with the gifts of grace. Acceptance of the Incarnation is the key to understanding humanity.

The next indispensable element in a Catholic culture is the concept of sacramentality. There is, in other words, a specific way in which God relates to people through time and space. Here the idea that the human person is composed of both spirit and matter and that God relates to both, not just to the spirit, is important. In the sacrament of the Eucharist the mere matter of bread and wine is changed into Christ's body and blood. Speaking of this moment, Ratzinger says: "the substantial conversion of bread and wine into His body and blood introduces within creation the principle of a radical change, a sort of 'nuclear fission,' which penetrates to the heart of all being."[1]

The sacraments, as the word suggests, sacralize human life. They raise it to a higher level. They are also one of the means by which a person receives grace. They are not simply social milestone markers.

A further indispensable element of a Catholic culture is the ability to distinguish authentic Christianity from its various secularist mutations. A common temptation in the present era is for people to try to separate the fruits of Christianity from belief in the basic tenets of the faith as expressed in the Creed. For example, kindness, patience, putting other people first, caring for one's neighbor are all fruits of a Christian culture. Secular humanists are often keen to retain these fruits but separate them from belief in God. This project leads to what Ratzinger calls "political moralism." In the absence of a strong Christian culture the state begins to act as if it were the Church: bureaucrats, especially Education Department bureaucrats, set themselves up in a position analogous to priests. As an alternative to a Christian moral formation they offer various social engineering policies. We end up in the absurd situation where children as young as four are monitored for so-called sexist behavior.

Many of Ratzinger's publications, including the encyclical *Spe Salvi*, offer critiques of the new secular morality, while his encyclical *Deus Caritas Est* can be read as a Catholic response to the Nietzschean charge that Christianity poisoned *eros*. Ratzinger does not deny that warped, Puritanical versions of Christianity denigrated *eros*. However he distinguishes a

[1] Benedict XVI, *Sacramentum Caritatis*, Paragraph 11, 2007.

Catholic account of sexuality which links *eros* to *agape* from those aberrant forms. He thereby provides further support for John Paul II's *Catechesis on Human Love*.

This is just a short list of the many elements of an embattled Catholic culture that can be found in the mountains of publications by Ratzinger.

The discovery of Ratzinger by future generations may well lead them on to the literary and philosophical treasures of his Polish friend Wojtyła and the theology of his Swiss friend von Balthasar, his French friend de Lubac, his Italian friend Giussani, and an English author called John Henry Newman. They may even find Tolkien and some hermit from the Orkneys called Mackay Brown, the Norwegian Nobel laureate Sigrid Undset and an Etonian called George from the noble house of Spencer who thought that there needed to be a prayer crusade for the restoration of the old faith in the UK.

Through these authors, a generation tired of the banality of cheap intimacy and nominalism gone mad may rediscover the buried capital of a civilization built on the belief that the Incarnation really did happen. They may also gradually learn to distinguish a secularized Christianity that hooked itself up to whatever *Zeitgeist* wafted along from the real mysteries celebrated in something called the old Christian calendar.

14

From Rockhampton to Rome

MY EARLIEST CHILDHOOD MEMORY OF the Catholic faith was of visiting St Brigid's Convent in Rockhampton. In those days, in the early 1960s, there was quite a large community of Mercy Sisters living in the convent. They ran a primary school, a hostel for single women, and a nursing home.

I was about to start school at St Mary's College in Ipswich even though I was an Anglican. My grandmother was very concerned about me turning up at a Catholic school knowing only Anglican prayers. She took me to meet the Mother Superior of St Brigid's, a lady called Mother de Chantel, who gave me a prayer book which had a picture of a guardian angel on the cover, escorting two children across a broken bridge.

Being an Anglican at a convent school was like going on an adventure in a foreign country. Although the new vernacular Order of the Mass had just been introduced, we were still taught Latin hymns, there was Benediction every first Friday, there were very solemn school Masses once a week and the Angelus was recited every day at noon. There were also feast days and fast days with the associated variations in food on offer at the tuck shop. We learned about saints and we collected "holy cards" that were bookmarks bearing the image of a saint. We were often given these as a reward for getting high marks and we would swap them among ourselves. For example, someone who had two St. Joseph's could swap a St. Joseph for a St George. Today when I am visiting churches in Europe I can usually work out the identity of the saints in their artwork from the education I

Published in Annals Australasia *in two parts, November–December 2015, and January–February 2016.*

received from those holy cards. They gave me a Catholic iconography 101 lesson.

The fact that I was an Anglican came out in grade 2 when I handed in a very sad project book. The project was called "My Family" and we were supposed to paste in a picture of the pope and our local archbishop and our parish priests, then our grandparents, parents, godparents and siblings. The general idea was to help us to understand that we belonged to a spiritual family that included not only our biological relatives but people like the pope, the archbishop, and others entrusted with our spiritual care.

I was an only child being brought up by a camera-shy grandmother. No one in my family purchased Catholic newspapers. As a consequence my project book consisted of only two photographs on a single page. One was a photograph of myself and the other was a picture of Pope Paul VI my grandmother cut out of a secular newspaper.

I was in the odd position of being top of my class for catechism but not actually Catholic. I found the intellectual side of the faith intriguing and I especially loved the way that time and eternity seemed to be fused together in the culture of the school, something that I would only later come to understand to be the result of a very sacramental cosmology.

My grandmother, who never had a problem with the papacy, only with Irish Republicans, agreed that I could become a Catholic and she made the necessary arrangements. I was accepted into full communion with the Catholic Church at the baptismal font in St. Mary's Church in Ipswich, surrounded by all of my classmates.

After four years at St. Mary's, I moved to Rockhampton where I attended Our Lady's Cathedral school, and then finally I went onto the Range Convent. My entire twelve years at school had been governed by the Sisters of Mercy.

I was recently at a dinner with the Trustees of the University of Notre Dame. The Vice-Chancellor of the University, Professor Celia Hammond, went to a Loreto school. One of the trustees joked that the difference between Loreto girls and Mercy girls is that Mercy girls grow up wanting to be doctors, and Loreto girls grow up wanting to marry doctors. Celia protested that this was an unfair caricature. Whatever the truth about Loreto girls, my experience of being a Mercy girl was one of a twelve-year apprenticeship on tightly-run ships.

I went through the system during an era when in primary school we had exams every month and we changed desks after every exam so that we were always sitting in academic rank order. The A students were in the back row and the weakest students in the front row and everyone in between was seated according to their latest exam results. There was homework to be memorized every night and the following morning we were tested. Stamps were placed in our exercise books if we got 100%. There was an angel with a halo around its head and 100% printed underneath. A week of 100% stamps gave a girl the right to a special merit stamp on Friday mornings. There was also a stamp featuring a tail-less donkey with the words "good work but where's the rest?" This was for slow students who got everything they attempted right, but didn't manage to finish the exercise.

I can remember our entire class chanting the phrase "dear God, help me not to be an imbecile" after we had all collectively fallen short of some standard of conduct. I was so often in trouble I concluded that the problem was my red hair. It made me stand out like a deer with a target painted on its chest.

In this context my strongest memory is of being summoned to the principal's office along with a number of other girls. We had committed the sin of playing football with the boys. No one ever told us that it was wrong to play football because it never

79

occurred to any of us to do so, until one day when Bishop Rush came into our playground. His home was a five minute walk from the school and from time to time he would just appear and play with us. On this day he started playing football with the boys, but their football kept running into the girls' netball game, and so we gave up playing netball and joined the football game with the bishop and the boys. When we arrived in the principal's office my defense was that the bishop was playing with us and he clearly thought it was perfectly okay.

It was at this moment that I learned a very important lesson in ecclesial life — that nuns are often more powerful than bishops. I found myself in extra trouble for being insubordinate and the merit of my defense was never addressed.

On the final day of primary school I was handed my report card by the same principal who said that she had been harder on me than on some of my classmates because she thought that I might "one day amount to something." She told my grandmother that she had to do a bit of pruning to sort out the defects in my character.

In secondary school I was blessed with a couple of teachers who decided to push a group of us to excel academically. Instead of expecting us to perform at the highest level of someone in our age group, we were given assessment tasks at a higher level. For example, we were writing argumentative essays in year 10, when that ability was not normally expected until year 12. We were also given university level biology texts when we were doing years 9 and 10 science. Whether we had an aptitude for music, or mathematics, or in my case the humanities subjects, we were given special attention and different assessment tasks. The girl who was the dux of our year majored in mathematics and then went to work for NASA, the North American Space Authority, the girl who came a close second is now a leading obstetrician and gynecologist in Sydney, and I ended up a theology professor.

Very significantly, in my generation this quest for excellence was not tied to any feminist ideology. It did, I think, have a little bit to do with sectarian rivalry. In other words, our teachers certainly hoped that we would get higher tertiary entrance scores than the girls at the Anglican school down the road. However at a deeper level this desire to get the best out of us was rooted in a theology which took seriously the proposition that from those to whom much has been given, much will be expected. The same nun who told my grandmother that I needed to be pruned told me that if I ever abandoned my faith she would come back from the dead and haunt me. The things she cared about were all theological.

Her basic message was that God gives grace and God gives talents. What we do with the grace and the talent is our free choice. But if we don't use these gifts for the glory of God, but for some lower purpose, like self-promotion, then there will be a day of reckoning. The people who have been given the greatest gifts will be the ones in the scariest positions at the general judgment.

The nuns also tried to prepare us for the battles with evil forces we were likely to encounter in adult life. To use a *Lord of the Rings* metaphor, they knew about orcs and they wanted to prepare us to be useful participants in the battles for Middle Earth. Or to use a *Harry Potter* metaphor, they saw themselves as being in the business of educating aurors. They didn't want us to sit around brushing our hair while our prince-husbands did all the fighting.

One of the scariest battles I ever faced was as a doctoral student in Cambridge. I found myself in the Department for Social and Political Sciences, a bureaucratic creation of the Vice-Chancellor in the late 1960s. He took all the Marxists out of the humanities departments and quarantined them in one new super department called the Department for Social and

Political Sciences, or simply "SPS." I wanted to work on the ideas of the Catholic political philosopher Alasdair MacIntyre so the Research Office parked me in the SPS faculty. I soon discovered that the Head of the Faculty was a personal enemy of Alasdair MacIntyre. They had been friends in the 1960s when they were both young radicals, but the friendship soured when MacIntyre started to get interested in Aquinas. By the time I arrived in the SPS faculty it was impossible to write a thesis that was in any way favorable to the ideas of Alasdair MacIntyre.

I was eventually summoned to a meeting with MacIntyre's nemesis. He began by saying that he didn't believe in God, that he didn't know anyone in Cambridge who believed in God, but he understood that this was a sociological phenomenon found in some parts of the United States and Poland. He suggested that I should be a student in one of those places. As I left his study knowing that he was determined to block my registration as a doctoral student I said a prayer to the now deceased Sister of Mercy who had dared to tell my grandmother that I had character defects. One day later the atheist professor had a massive heart attack. He didn't die but he was in intensive care for several weeks. During that time I got out of the SPS Faculty and into the Divinity school where all was plain sailing. I worked under the direction of Professor John Milbank, a high church Anglican and friend of Dr Rowan Williams, the former Archbishop of Canterbury. It is now a joke in academic theology circles that Milbank was running a "witness protection service" in Cambridge, shielding all kinds of theistic students from the political correctness police. Some of us were Catholic, others Anglican, there was one Anabaptist and one Jew. What we all had in common was that we had run into trouble with people who thought that there is no place for God in Cambridge. This is notwithstanding the fact that without the Catholic Church there would be no Cambridge, and indeed for that matter, no Oxford, no Sorbonne, no Jagiellonian, no universities of Bologna, Granada, St. Andrews, Edinburgh, Leipzig, Vienna, Salamanca, Toulouse, Aberdeen, Siena, Padua, Glasgow, or Basel, all of which were founded either by Catholic clerics or by Catholic monarchs. The university, like the hospital, is very much an institution of Christendom.

Some years later I found myself on a panel at a conference in Rome with Professor Milbank and I said to him, "if it wasn't for you rescuing me from the SPS Faculty, I would not be sitting here now." He smiled and said, "you and about a dozen others." He then went on to speak proudly of a number of other doctoral students who had gone on to have successful academic careers who had run up against people who tried to torpedo them because they didn't want believing Christians to hold positions of authority in academic institutions.

Universities are what the Italian Marxist Antonio Gramsci called "switch points of cultural power." Gramsci argued that in developed Western countries, unlike in rural countries such as 19th-century Russia or 1940s China, the way to bring about a Marxist revolution is not to go about firing guns and herding people into gulags. Rather he encouraged Marxists to gain control of the switch points of cultural power, meaning the newspapers, all forms of media outlets, schools, and above all, the universities. In short, if you control the world of ideas, you control the culture. Most sociologists now agree that the intellectual radicals of the generation of 1968, what the French call the *soixante-huitards*, did indeed take control of the universities in the 1970s, and what we are living through today, in terms of social engineering policies, is the political "fruit," so to speak, of the ideological cocktails of the generation of 1968.

For example, we hear a lot about gender theory today, and many Catholics find it hard to understand how they could suddenly wake up in a world where, according to Facebook, there are over 50 different gender orientations if you are an American, and over 70 if you are British. But back in the 1980s I was taught by a lecturer at the University of Queensland who, when asked whether his partner had given birth to a girl or a boy, would reply, "it is up to the child to decide its gender orientation." His children were given unisex names and no one was allowed to speak of them as girls or boys because to do so was to oppress them with a premodern paradigm.

What sounds like a crazy idea to one generation can start to gain traction as something normal if a critical mass of academics start to push the idea.

The English writer G. K. Chesterton was onto the problem when he wrote that the Catholic Church is the only thing that stands between the human being and the indignity of being a child of one's time. By this he meant that a proper Catholic intellectual formation gives one a framework by which to judge passing intellectual fashions.

There is an old adage that the fashion of a decade is rarely, if ever, the truth of a century. For example, nationalism was fashionable in the second decade of the twentieth century, but totally out of favor by the end of the 20th century. Fascism was fashionable with some in the 1930s but by 1945 most people had had enough of it. Marxism was fashionable in the 1960s but in 1989 when the Berlin Wall came down, being a Marxist suddenly became really unfashionable and almost overnight it became the norm to describe oneself as a "postmodern."

Only if Catholic children are given a proper intellectual formation and a proper formation of the heart can they resist becoming nuts and bolts in ideological machines.

My auror training in Mercy schools had been effective and I survived my battle with an atheist Cambridge professor. On the day of my doctoral defense I passed him in the courtyard of King's College. He didn't recognize me, but we crossed paths walking in opposite directions and I said a prayer of thanksgiving to all those in heaven who had worked on my case.

On the basis of my doctorate from the Cambridge Divinity School which had been funded by the British foreign office under its scheme for scholarships for students from Commonwealth countries, I became the inaugural Dean of the John Paul II Institute in Melbourne. The first session of the Institute, located at the Lateran University in Rome, was personally founded by St John Paul II on the 13th of May in 1981, the day of the assassination attempt on his life. He was leaving St Peter's square to travel to the Lateran University for the opening ceremony when the assassination attempt took place.

His idea was to have several sessions of the Institute located around the world, all affiliated to the Roman session and offering a common core curriculum of theological anthropology and moral and sacramental theology, with different sessions offering their own additional specializations. In the case of the Australian session the specializations became bioethics, catechetics, and the theology of culture, which is really a subfield of theological anthropology.

Since the Melbourne Institute is affiliated to the Roman John Paul II Institute which has Pontifical status, I was required to obtain the additional pontifical degrees, the STL or Licentiate in Sacred Theology, and the comically named STD or Doctorate in Sacred Theology.

The first Director of the Melbourne affiliated session of the Institute, Fr Anthony Fisher, who is now Archbishop Fisher of Sydney, was also told that he had to get the two pontifical degrees, because his doctorate was from Oxford, and Oxford, like Cambridge, cut its ties to the papacy during the Reformation.

Fr Fisher procrastinated, or at least gave priority to other jobs, and then when he was made a bishop he was told that he no longer needed the pontifical degrees because as a bishop he is given an honorary DD, or doctorate in divinity, which comes with the purple socks, without having to write a single sentence. A DD trumps an STD.

I, however, had no such loophole to exploit. I had to write a 40,000 word Licentiate dissertation and an 80,000 word second doctoral dissertation. Archbishop Hart kindly gave me a week's extra annual leave to write the doctoral dissertation. As I sat before a bench of five professors at the Lateran University and answered questions which were delivered in three different languages, the Chairman said, "you know Professor Rowland, if you were a bishop, we would not need to do this."

In 2014, I was appointed to the International Theological Commission, a body which was founded by Pope Paul VI. It is a kind of think tank comprised of 30 theologians who are appointed for five year terms and work under the supervision of the Prefect for the Congregation of the Doctrine of the Faith (the "CDF"). The thirty theologians work on three documents over the course of their five-year term and the documents are on topics chosen by the ITC members themselves. The current topics are: religious liberty, the powers of synods, and the relationship between faith and sacramentality.

When I first sat in the ITC's meeting room beside Cardinal Müller it did feel a very long way from the baptismal font in St. Mary's, the playground of Our Lady's with Bishop Rush and stray footballs, and the library of the Range Convent where I had beavered away on hot afternoons.

Rome is awesome and Rome can also be comically mad. One of the awesome aspects is the weight of history that hovers over the whole city. It is hard to go there and feel arrogant. Instead one has a sense that St. Peter's Square really is the fulcrum around which the entire history of the world turns and one feels extremely privileged to play any part in that history — just being a common no-brand sheep is itself a privilege.

There is also a sense of being at home in Rome, of belonging, in the same way that the African nun standing at the same traffic light belongs and is right at home and the Japanese priest eating gelato under a palm tree is right at home, and the American parents with a couple of boys in Swiss Guard or Roman centurion outfits, are right at home. It is a place where deep friendships can be made in a matter of minutes because two people quickly realize that they believe and love and have dedicated their lives to the same things.

Nonetheless, as in all families, individuals have their own temperaments and idiosyncrasies. The Roman meetings bring together people from every nation on the planet, and the national idiosyncrasies are obvious. The French are usually the best dressed and have the most sophisticated manners, and somewhere in their presentations there will be a reference to the ongoing significance of the French Revolution. The Germans are usually the most highly educated, the Poles the most romantic in the sense of idealistic, the British the most polite and understated, the Australians the least reverential of authority figures, the Americans the worst at foreign languages but they make up for this by being generous with their money, buying coffee and lunch for others.

At the academic conferences there are very real differences between the Latinos and people from the Anglosphere. Our academic cultures are very different. People coming from a British background think that they need to say something original in their papers because at our universities we don't pass our doctorates unless we have something original to say. However the typical caricature of someone with an educational background in Latin America is that they spend the first third of their paper praising the chairman of their panel, the middle third summarizing the Church's teaching in a given area, and the final section demonstrating that the Church's

87

teaching is consistent with Plato or Aristotle, or if they are a liberation theologian, with the Puebla statement. The typical Anglophone speaker says thank you to the chairman and then moves directly to the point of his or her presentation which is usually the identification of some pastoral problem which is then analyzed by reference to numerous academic sources, not all of which stem from the Church's own scholarship, and then some attempt is made to offer an original solution to the pastoral problem identified.

In his book *The Gothic Fox and the Baroque Hedgehog*, Claudio Veliz offered an extensive analysis of the difference between the Spanish and English mental universe, using Isaiah Berlin's category of the Gothic Fox to signify the British outlook and the Baroque Hedgehog to signify the Spanish. The fox is more flexible than the hedgehog. The hedgehogs view the world through the lens of a single defining idea, the foxes draw on a wide variety of experiences.

On one occasion when giving a paper in Rome I found myself in the middle of a cultural misunderstanding typical of the difference between the perspective of a Fox and a Hedgehog. Acting like a fox, I gave a paper in which I cited Rowan Williams who was then the Anglican Archbishop of Canterbury. He had recently been inducted into a Welsh Honorary Society called the Welsh Gorsedd of Bards. To be initiated into the Society he had to go through a ceremony dressed as a Welsh Druid and photographs of the Archbishop so dressed were published all over the world, including in Spain. After I completed my paper a Spanish professor approached my superior and suggested that I be dismissed from my position because it was unthinkable that a member of the John Paul II Institute could be endorsing Druidism. Bishop Peter Elliott came to my defense and tried to explain that although Rowan Williams had recently been photographed dressed as a Druid, this does not mean that he

is, theologically speaking, a Druid. The Gorsedd of Bards is
an honorary society for people who have made distinguished
contributions to the Welsh language and culture, and like most
gentlemen's clubs in the Anglophone world, when you join
them there is an initiation ceremony evocative of initiation
ceremonies at British all-male boarding schools. In this case,
Williams had to dress up like a Druid. Bishop Elliott is himself a
former Anglican and his explanations were not very persuasive.
I was ultimately defended by a Spanish priest who had worked
in Washington for several years and thus had some idea about
Anglophone cultures. He testified that to the best of his personal
experience, I was not a Druid, and he suggested that in order
to understand how an Anglican Archbishop could dress up as
a Druid and stand in a field with other men dressed as Druids,
without actually being a Druid, one needed to be born British.

Being accused of being a Druid is not however my maddest
Roman experience. That occurred only last year. I was with
other members of the International Theological Commission
in a room in the papal palace. We were there to be formally
presented to the pope. Cardinal Pell had warned me that the
pope has very little English and therefore he suggested that
I prepare something to say in Italian or German. I took the
German option. When the pope got to me he had Cardinal
Müller at his side. I said about 4 sentences in perfect German
to the effect that the students of the Institute in Melbourne
are praying for the pope. I could see Cardinal Müller beaming
with pride as I used his own mother tongue. Müller then said
to the pope, "Professor Rowland hat zwei Söhne" (Professor
Rowland has two sons). I replied "nein, ich habe kein Söhnen"
(No, I have no sons). Müller then says, "sie haben Tochter" (You
have daughters)! I say "Nein, ich habe kein Kinder" (No, I have
no children). Müller then says, "you are a consecrated virgin?"
And then I said, still in German, "no, I am married but I do

not have any children." At this point I remember that Sr Prudence Allen, a Sister of Mercy who was standing right beside me dressed in a long habit to her ankles and almost an equally long veil, was once married and she had two sons before joining the Sisters of Mercy. I say to the pope and Cardinal Müller, "it is Sr Prudence who has two sons." Müller and the pope both exchanged "she is completely daft" looks, Müller then made a gesture with his hands meaning no way, impossible, and then he steered the pope onto Sr Prudence before I could dig myself into a deeper hole.

When we got out of the meeting Sr Prudence turned to me and said, "That was so funny, Tracey, Cardinal Müller had obviously confused our CVs." I felt like saying, well, you could have bailed me out, you could have acknowledged that you are the one with the sons, habit and veil notwithstanding, but having been brought up by an Anglican grandma, I reserved my judgement and entertained Buddhist thoughts about how Dr Karma would no doubt get her back at some future time.

In addition to these completely mad moments there have also been many charming and beautiful experiences, like being photographed with the Vatican cat whose name is Zoro because he has a black patch over one eye. He lives in the Vatican gardens and is a regular visitor to Pope Benedict's monastery. I have also met many really saintly people and have been privileged to sit with them at lunch and learn about the heroism of Catholics in other parts of the world.

Obviously, one doesn't have to be a scholar to be a good Catholic, but throughout the whole 2,000-year history of the Church there have always been people in every generation who have made the intellectual life of the Church their special form of ecclesial service. Without them there would have been no monastic libraries, no great universities, and a rather large amount of confusion.

It is often said that to think like a Catholic is to avoid dualisms. For example, the Calvinist theologian Karl Barth said in a famous paragraph that Catholics are rather taken with the word "and." Where Protestants say Jesus, Catholics say "Jesus and Mary." Where Protestants seek to obey Christ, Catholics want to obey Christ and his Vicar on earth, the Pope. While Protestants believe the Christian is saved through the merits of Jesus Christ, Catholics want to add, "and our own merits," that is, because of our works. While Protestants believe the sole source of Revelation is found in Scripture, Catholics want to add "and Tradition." While Protestants say knowledge of God is obtained by faith in His Word expressed in Scripture, Catholics want to add "and by reason," and so on.

Arguably there is another dualism that Barth did not name and that is the dualism between hierarchy and democracy. Calvinism is very democratic and the Catholic faith has its own democratic elements. But the Catholic faith also has a hierarchical element and this means that we don't accept that one person's theological opinion is as good as the next person's. There is the idea that we have to actually know the Catholic tradition in some depth before we can go about saying what it is and what it should be, and this is a hierarchical element. It means that education is important.

However, when the Church is functioning well it should not matter whether one grows up in the 5th or 7th arrondissement of Paris with all of its cultural sophistication or somewhere north of Nambour, because in all places there will be a strong respect for intellectual work and encouragement for those who show academic promise. This is because Catholics believe that even after the Fall, or what the French call the "original catastrophe," the image of God in the human soul has not been effaced, and the work of the intellect is potentially one of the fruits of our relationship to God. Any kind of anti-intellectualism, born of the fear that intellectual formation might encourage elitism, is a most uncatholic way of thinking. Instead, we do our best to develop the gifts that God has given to those we meet in life and we hope that they will use their gifts and the education they receive through the ministry of the Church for the glory of God.

15

Obituary for
Sr Patrice Kennedy RSM

THIS MORNING I RECEIVED A CALL FROM
Fr John Grace, the Administrator of the Diocese of
Rockhampton, in the state of Queensland in northern
Australia. I imagine that the closest American equivalent would
be the Diocese of Fort Worth. Queensland is a little like Texas
in the Pacific. It's a state that runs on the beef cattle industry
and produces a large amount of the nation's mineral wealth.

Fr Grace called to tell me that Sr Patrice Kennedy RSM
had died on Sunday evening. She was a Sister of Mercy, in her
80s, who had joined the Order in Galway when she was still
a teenager. It's hard to imagine the state of mind of a teenage
girl in the 1940s deciding to commit to a life of celibacy and
the prospect of never seeing one's family and country again.

Like Texas, there are large chunks of the Diocese of Rockhampton that are sparsely populated, arid plains. A train line
connects the provincial city of Rockhampton with its population of 109,000 to towns like Blackwater, Emerald, Barcaldine,
Longreach, and Mt. Isa. The towns service the mining and
cattle industries of the "outback," which means miles and miles
of red dust, ant hills, spinifex grass and the occasional mob of
kangaroos. It is also the natural habitat of snakes that can kill
in a matter of minutes and other reptiles like goannas. The
topography is often compared to that of Israel: little settlements
surrounded by desert, where the days are scorching hot but the
temperatures plummet at night. At certain times of the year
Min Min lights appear. These are a kind of mirage caused by

Published in the Sydney Catholic Weekly, February 2013.

rays of light being bent when they pass through air layers of different temperatures. Seeing a Min Min can be a very eerie experience. They tend to follow cars and animals as if they were spirits with intentionality. The indigenous Australians had all kinds of legends about them.

It was to these outback towns with their assortment of deadly animals, Min Min lights, and tough minded individuals that Sr Patrice and other Irish girls of her generation came to serve the Catholic people.

She found herself teaching in classrooms of over 40 children and she gained a reputation for being a good coach of the boys' football team. I first met her in 1973 when she was preparing my class for Confirmation. Every morning she would ask the question, "Who went to Mass this morning?" and a forest of hands would go up. This was because she spent a lot of time explaining to us how important the Eucharist is, and how lucky we were that we could go to Mass every day whereas children who had to live behind the Iron Curtain where often deprived of the sacraments.

We began each class by curtsying to her and after that we would listen half-mesmerized by her Gaelic accent. Someone once described a friend of mine as a woman who could charm a room full of teenage boys into eschewing all forms of alcohol and devoting their lives to the welfare of lepers. Sr Patrice had that quality. We did whatever she wanted because we loved her.

At the time the principal of the school was Sr Mary Clotilde. "Chloe" was one of thirteen children from a cattle property in the outback and she ran an extremely tight ship. She believed in excellence in all things. Once a year, there was a sports carnival for all the Catholic primary schools, and she was so determined that her school would win that she made every child run laps around the cathedral before the first class of the day. Sr Patrice's job was to drive Sr Clotilde around the cathedral in the Kingswood — a type of Holden car iconic of 1970s Australia. Sr Clotilde would sit in the passenger's seat with a megaphone so she could call out to particular children, mention (or shame) them by name, and order them to pick up their feet and run harder. As a consequence, we did win the sports carnival.

The last time I saw Sr Patrice was in October. She had moved to a nursing home. When I arrived a nurse escorted me to her room and on the way she told me that Sr Patrice had lots of visitors who were former students. The nurse asked me what she had been like as a teacher, why was she so popular? I said that she wouldn't take any nonsense, but she was kind and loving and her smile could light up a corridor.

I began our conversation by asking Sr Patrice the names of people who had been to see her recently and she mentioned someone who runs a veterinary practice. I told her that my cat had gone on a hunger strike last Easter because I gave her some upmarket mince as an Easter treat and then she refused to go back to the cheaper food. I admitted that I was charged $68 by the vet to be told that the cat's problem was psychological. She gave me a very disappointed look. She thought I was a whole lot smarter than someone who could be taken for a ride by a cat. She did however suggest that in future if I needed a vet, I could go to her former student, mention her name, and get a "mate's rates" deal.

Of all the accolades that could be showered upon her, high on the list is the fact that in the chaos of the 60s and 70s, she never lost the plot. The faith and the love she had as a teenager never corrupted or dissipated. She was still as enthusiastic about her faith in 2013 as she was in 1973. She still had the lilt in her voice and the mischief in her eyes. She still believed in the same God. Until very recently she was driving a car to make parish visitations and interpreting traffic lights as mere recommendations.

People often joke that being born amidst the chaos of the 1960s is a "get out of jail" free card on the day of judgment. I fear however that anyone who was taught by Sr Patrice, and others like her, will be held to a higher standard. May she rest in eternal peace.

16

Pre-Moderns, Moderns, and Post-Moderns

I N 2006, I WAS INVITED TO DELIVER A paper at a conference at Baylor University in Waco, Texas. Baylor is a Protestant University that markets itself as the Harvard of the South. It is remarkable in that it has a student population of 18,000 but the campus is totally dry.

When I received the invitation to participate I was told that if I also delivered a homily at the student chaplaincy service, I would be paid an honorarium of $1,000. I immediately agreed to the deal without asking for further and better particulars.

At Australian universities, student chaplaincies are usually sad places for people without friends. I imagined I would have an audience of about a dozen lonely undergraduates. However when I arrived at the chaplaincy I discovered that I was to speak in an auditorium that seats 2,000, since attendance at a certain number of chaplaincy services is a mandatory requirement for getting a degree at Baylor. The university authorities enforce this regulation through a swipe card device. Every student has to swipe a card at a chaplaincy service a certain number of times each year.

I was then introduced to the chaplain who took me to a dressing room and prayed over me for several minutes. He then explained that when it was my time to deliver the homily a green light would start to flash and that would be my cue to come on stage.

The service began with a rock band singing Christian lyrics, and after about fifteen minutes of the rock group, the green

Address to a meeting of the Australian Catholic Students Association, Brisbane, 2009.

light started to flash. Just as I thought that the situation could not possibly be any more surreal, the chaplain invited the 2,000 or so students to welcome Dr Tracey Rowland all the way from Melbourne in the United Kingdom. (There may well be a Melbourne somewhere in the United Kingdom but the better known one is on Port Phillip Bay in Australia.) I then proceeded to deliver the least evangelical homily in Baylor's history, and my text on that occasion has been re-cast here.

I began by explaining the major fault lines in contemporary humanities scholarship between the pre-moderns, the moderns, and the post-moderns. In a nutshell the pre-moderns believe that faith and reason belong together, that the relationship between them is intrinsic. The moderns want to sever the relationship, exalt the faculty of reason, and privatize faith, and the post-moderns agree with the pre-moderns that there is an intrinsic relationship between faith and reason, but they reject the idea that the human intellect can actually discern that one faith is superior to another. To put it crudely, they reject the idea that we can intellectually discern that Christianity is superior to astrology.

This way of understanding the divisions within Arts Faculties across the Western world is taken largely from the works of Charles Taylor who is based at McGill University in Canada, and Alasdair MacIntyre, who is based at the University of Notre Dame in Indiana. Although they have their subtle differences, they both agree that the theists, and in particular the Catholic Church as an institution, are currently suffering a double-fronted attack: on the one side there are attacks influenced by 18th-century conceptions of rationality and human freedom, and on the other, there are the attacks coming from those influenced by 19th-century conceptions of freedom and rationality. In short-hand terms one can refer to the 18th-century rationalists and the 19th-century romantics, or more commonly, to the

18th-century moderns and the 19th-century post-moderns, the moderns being the rationalists obsessed with pure reason, and the post-moderns being the romantics, obsessed with lifestyle choice and social experimentation.

Taylor and MacIntyre trace the origins of these two fronts all the way back to developments in philosophy and theology in the 14th century. Suffice to say that from the 14th to 17th centuries Christendom suffered a spiritual and intellectual crisis which ended in revolutions and the division of Europe into Catholic and Protestant blocs. By the 18th century, members of the intellectual elite tired of this strife decided that the reasonable approach to life is to regard religion as something purely psychological and as such something that should have no public significance. Faith and reason should be severed into separate boxes and kept chastely apart. A philosophy based on what Immanuel Kant called "pure reason" was the only thing that could be the basis of public order. In German this was called *Aufklärung*, which was translated into English as Enlightenment.

Kant understood that if his project of defending morality by reference to reason alone failed, then there could be terrible social repercussions, and these repercussions did begin to unfold from at least the late nineteenth century onwards, and were given a strong impetus by the ideas of Friedrich Nietzsche (1844–1900).

Nietzsche not only thought that God was dead, but he thought Kantian rationality was dead too. Moreover, he didn't believe in a philosophical fiction like "human nature." He believed only in psychological drives. He divided society into two types of people: those who squash their own humanity by trying to make their drives operate within a Christian moral framework, these he called "members of the herd," and those who had the courage and audacity to live beyond Christian conceptions of good and evil. These he thought were the elite or *Übermenschen*.

99

Nietzsche was also in the tradition of the German Romantics. The Romantics saw life as an artistic enterprise and they wanted each and every life to have the properties of a great work of art, especially the quality of originality. They wanted art to replace the traditional role of religion as the incentive and stimulus for morality. They were interested in conceptions of truth, goodness, and beauty, but most of them wanted to replace a Christian conception of these with neo-pagan Greek conceptions. For many of the Romantics Christian culture had proved to be disappointing, and this was especially so for those who had found the Puritan spirit in German Protestantism oppressive.

Nietzsche believed that Christianity, though on the wane in European culture, would continue to be influential unless and until scholars turned their attack on Christian morality. Prior to Nietzsche there had been a tendency for scholars to focus their criticisms on apparent scientific inaccuracies in the Bible, but they had not directly attacked Christian morality. In 1888 in his work on the *Will to Power*, Nietzsche wrote:

> Up to the present the assault against Christianity has not only been fainthearted, it has been wide of the mark. So long as Christian Ethics are not felt to be a capital crime against life, their defenders will have the game in their hands. The problem of the 'truth' of Christianity—the existence of its God or the historicity of its legend, to say nothing of its astronomy and its natural science—is in itself a very subsidiary problem so long as the values of Christian ethics go unquestioned.

In the latter half of the twentieth century, especially from the late 1960s onwards, this Nietzschean dream has been in the process of being realized. It provides much of the intellectual infrastructure for what John Paul II called the culture of death and Pope Benedict calls the dictatorship of relativism.

In law schools and political science departments this dictatorship of relativism tends to be buttressed by what is called the theory of the "morally neutral state," or simply the "neutral state." The idea is that religion should be a purely private affair, it should have no public standing, and the state should not produce legislation covering the area of morals. If people want to have abortions, or produce embryos for experimentation, or children for homosexual couples, then this should be an acceptable practice because only those who believe that human life is sacred have a problem with it, and the belief that human life is sacred is a religious belief, that is, by definition, one that should have no public validity. Moral neutrality is thus a new political virtue.

One of its leading twentieth century proponents was the Harvard lawyer John Rawls. He argued that if a person wants to spend his life counting blades of grass, then that is a good life for him, and no one else has the right to question whether such a lifestyle is really desirable. In short, there are as many different ideas of the good as there are people, there is no absolute good, no ideal life, no objective morality. I don't know of any law school or political science department in the western world where *A Theory of Justice* is not mandatory reading, and if one reads the speeches on the life issues legislation in Hansard one finds frequent reference to the notion of the morally neutral state.

To date the major intellectual resistance to these ideas is coming from the post-moderns. The post-moderns reject the whole idea of pure reason and the possibility of a religiously neutral account of reality. They believe that all philosophies, all accounts of what is rational, all interpretations of what is real, are at root theological, or to use the more fashionable academic term, mythological, and that this is inescapable. From this the argument arose that proponents of 18th-century rationalism

were promoting social oppression because they were hiding
their theological prejudices behind the smoke screen of a secular rationality.

Catholics can agree with the post-modern conclusions
about the atheistic theological prejudice which lies behind the
smoke screen of a secular rationality, but where Catholics and
post-moderns differ is that Catholics believe that it is possible
to use their intellects to discern that one theological framework
is better than another one, that the myth of the Incarnation,
for example, is better than the myths of the classical Greeks,
the Romans, the Norsemen, the Druids, and contemporary
New Age therapists.

Thus Charles Taylor has summarized the Church's predicament in contemporary Western culture in the following words:

> There are secular humanists, there are neo-Nietzsche-
> ans and there are those who acknowledge some good
> beyond life. Any pair can gang up against the third
> on some important legal issue. Neo-Nietzscheans and
> secular humanists together condemn religion and
> reject any good beyond life. But neo-Nietzscheans
> and [theists] are together in their absence of sur-
> prise at the continued disappointments of secular
> humanism and together also in the sense that they
> observe that [the secular humanist] vision of life lacks
> a transcendent dimension. In a third line up, secular
> humanists and believers come together in defending
> an idea of the human good, against the anti-human-
> ism of Nietzsche's heirs. A fourth party can be intro-
> duced if we take into account the fact that theists are
> themselves divided.[1]

---

1 Charles Taylor, "Die immanente Gegenaufklärung," in *Aufklärung heute*,
ed. Krzystof Michalski (Stuttgart: Klett-Cotta, 1997).

In other words, the Catholic Church ends up under attack for trying to defend her understanding of human dignity within the public realm because the 18th-style rationalists argue that religion has no place in public life, while the 19th-century romantic Nietzschean types regard Catholic conceptions of human dignity and human freedom as oppressive, since they set limits on the freedom of the individual to construct his or her life as a work of art.

Whereas Karl Marx thought of the ideal man as someone who could hunt in the morning, fish after lunch, and rear cattle in the evening, the ideal post-modern is someone who is heterosexual in the morning, homosexual after lunch and bi-sexual in the evening. For the post-moderns, nothing, not even human nature, or a person's sexual orientation, is something constant. Everything is, or should be, possible. As a consequence, it is a complete waste of time trying to defend the Church's teachings to a post-modern by reference to the idiom of natural law, which presupposes some constant like human nature, or to the rhetoric of rights, which is usually based on some form of Kantian jurisprudence which they reject as yet another case of theological prejudices masquerading as a secular rationality.

So the first major point I made to the students at Baylor is that regardless of what they believe about God, if they are to have an intellectual life or to make a significant contribution to public life, then they will need to acquaint themselves with these contemporary intellectual and cultural cleavages. As Alasdair MacIntyre expresses the point, every major social institution in the Western world, but particularly our universities, our courts, and our parliaments, are a site of civil war between proponents of these various frameworks.

The second point I made is that of all the frameworks on offer in the marketplace of ideas, the Christian framework is the only one that is based on the idea that God is love and this point has become the signature tune of the papacy of Benedict XVI. Whereas John Paul II spent quite a bit of time on the faith and reason relationship, Benedict XVI has expanded the framework into a faith and reason and love relationship.

Both Wojtyła and Ratzinger have understood that beneath all the intellectual assaults with which the Church is daily confronted, there is a conflict about the nature of the human person, and it is precisely for this reason that so many of the encyclicals of the past quarter century have dealt with anthropological issues. They understand that what we are up against is not something as simple as poor philosophy but competing conceptions of what it means to be a human being.

In the first three encyclicals of his pontificate Benedict XVI has therefore emphasized the highly personal nature of God, and the fact that Christianity is not an ethical framework, but about being in a relationship with the Trinity, especially Christ, who, as the Second Person of the Trinity, represents humanity as it was intended to be. This is essentially the idea expressed in paragraph 22 of the conciliar document *Gaudium et Spes*, which was the paragraph of the Second Vatican Council most often cited in the speeches and homilies of John Paul II.

Pope Benedict has also tried in each of his encyclicals to emphasize the social nature of salvation. He is highly critical of the mentality that sees salvation as a kind of project to be undertaken by individuals who try to notch up spiritual credit on an imaginary report card or eternal curriculum vitae. He calls this sort of attitude "pious pelagianism." On the other hand he is critical of the mentality that nothing we do really matters so long as we are well intentioned, that the call to spiritual perfection could not really have been meant for everyone. He calls this "bourgeois pelagianism."

As a general sociological observation, one can say that people who care about matters of private morality are more likely to err by being pious pelagians, while those who care more about social justice and are less concerned about the private morality issues, are more likely to err in the direction of bourgeois pelagianism. The important point is that one of Pope Benedict's key concerns is to overcome this dualism between private morality and social justice.

Thus in *Deus Caritas Est*, his first encyclical, he made it clear that the Church's charitable activity is no optional extra but something as fundamental as a manifestation of Trinitarian love. He said that this command to love one's neighbor is inscribed by the Creator in the very nature of the human person. He also noted that Christian charity is essentially different from other forms of social welfare. While professional competence is a fundamental requirement of the work of Christians in charitable institutions, it is not alone sufficient. Christian love should transform the very ethos, the fundamental practices, of Christian institutions. In practice this means that Catholic schools should not be just like government schools with an extra class called religious education, and Catholic hospitals should not be just like government sponsored hospitals with the occasional crucifix, statue, or prayer space added. This is because Christian love, if authentic, changes everything. In philosophical language, it makes an ontological difference. In his second encyclical *Spe Salvi*, he stated that it was not science but love that redeems man. In *Caritas in Veritate* he argued that "a humanism which excludes God is an inhuman humanism" and that "life in Christ is the first and principal factor of all human development." The whole document is a plea to understand the limitations of a secularist notion of development. Behind secularism lies the error of Pelagius, which in contemporary times takes the form of trust in concepts like democracy, or human rights without reference to God or the interior dynamics of the human soul. A purely secularist notion of development reduces the human person to a kind of economic machine somehow designed for the accumulation of wealth.

Such a truncated concept of development has fostered government policies hostile or at least indifferent to the more spiritual elements of human life, while such secularist notions of development fail to comprehend the root cause of drug addiction and depression, which is the malnutrition of the human soul, made for communion with God but imprisoned within a materialist universe. When cultures no longer serve the deepest needs of human nature and actually narrow the spiritual horizons of people, people don't know who they are and feel depressed.

In his encyclical *Caritas in Veritate*, Benedict XVI suggests that the remedy for this pandemic in contemporary Western culture is to grasp the fact that truth is something which is given to us as a gift: "In every cognitive process, truth is not something that we produce, it is always found, or better, received. Truth, like love, is neither planned nor willed, but somehow imposes itself upon human beings."

Having thus identified the broad intellectual contours of the battlefield, those of you of a more practical disposition are likely to want some strategic plan for action. Unfortunately I don't have one of those, just a few general points:

1. As Catholics we need to do a better job of educating our youth, so that they at least understand the political and cultural contexts in which they find themselves. Every senior level student in a Catholic school should have at least a rudimentary acquaintance with the history of ideas from the 18th century to the present, with a special emphasis on the difference between a Catholic worldview and a post-modern worldview. For certain, as a matter of logic, if they begin to think like post-moderns, refusing to use their intellects to make value judgments, they will abandon their faith.

2. As Catholics involved in public life we need to develop some more sophisticated intellectual strategies for presenting our conceptions of human dignity and human freedom. We can't rely on old formulas like the right to life or the natural moral law, which have proven to be totally ineffectual and simply don't have anything to say to people who don't believe in God or a created order in the world.

In this context, Benedict XVI believes that a new ruling class is arising in the Western world which is running on Nietzschean principles. The Nietzschean virtues are those of power and self-sufficiency, the ability to compete and get ahead of others, and pursue whatever lifestyle one desires; the Christian virtues are the exact opposite, humility, love of our neighbor, self-sacrifice for the good of friends and family, and a lifestyle which in some form follows Christ.

Ratzinger is of the view that if the underlying attitudes to love in the various competing frameworks are drawn out into the open, then the Christian alternative will start to appear more attractive. In other words, it might be better to try to defend our pro-life values by reference to love rather than rights or other explicitly political rhetoric. For example pro-life movements in the United States have discovered that they get much further when they present their case with reference to the emotional and social predicament of the mother than if they focus on the rights of the embryo. What is called the Pro-Woman approach to the problem of the abortion industry is also the one recommended by John Paul II in his encyclical *Evangelium Vitae*.

3. Thirdly, Nietzsche once made the point that if Christians want to be taken seriously, then they need to at least *look* as though they have been redeemed. It is in part for this reason that Benedict XVI is spending so much effort talking about beauty and trying to reform the liturgy. If our own cultural life

is refined and edifying and not pitched to the lowest common denominator, not leveled down to meet the standards of the most illiterate person in the pew, then we might start to look as though we have been redeemed. We might then begin to offer a viable alternative to the kinds of lifestyle experiments pursued by the post-moderns; and we won't have to bribe our students to attend Mass and enforce the regulations by installing swipe card machines.

We will only win the political battles if we reclaim the culture for Christ, and we can only do that if we attend to the intellectual formation of our youth.

17

Eulogy for
Professor Nicholas Tonti-Filippini

PROFESSOR NICHOLAS TONTI-FILIPPINI
was an Australian bioethicist who suffered from an
auto-immune disease for most of his adult life. He was
a Professor of Bioethics at the John Paul II Institute in Melbourne,
a Knight in Obedience of the Sovereign Military Order of St. John
of Jerusalem, Rhodes and Malta, as well as a Knight of St. Gregory, and he was posthumously awarded the Order of Australia.

Nicholas was the only member of the original full-time faculty of the Melbourne session of the Institute who didn't have
a doctorate from one of the prestigious British universities. He
once explained to me that because of his illness he could not
obtain an overseas scholarship. Instead he put himself through
the most intellectually rigorous training possible in Australia,
including, for a time, working under the research supervision
of the utilitarian philosopher Peter Singer, the person who is
famous for supporting such practices as infanticide and sexual
intimacy with pets. In other words, Nicholas chose to work
under the academic supervision of someone who held ideas
that stood in dramatic contrast to that of his own. He believed
that in this way he would sharpen his intellectual skills.

He survived this intellectual ordeal and it gave him an
unshakeable belief in the power of dialectics. He thought that
if people's ideas were subjected to rigorous analysis and shown
to be flawed they would have to concede the point. This meant

---

*Speech delivered at the reception following the Requiem Mass
for the repose of the soul of Professor Nicholas Tonti-Filippini, St.
Patrick's Cathedral, Archdiocese of Melbourne, November 18, 2014.*

in turn that he thrived on debate. He once told us that when he was growing up in a family of ten children his father would turn the evening meal into a debating contest by taking the opposite opinion to that of his children and seeing if they could argue their case. Nicholas would look quite genuinely baffled if we tried to explain to him that some people support ideas for *non-intellectual* reasons—for example, for political reasons, or for reasons of upward social mobility, or reasons of the heart. This way of operating was completely foreign to him.

Because he so strongly believed that a good argument could uncover the truth, he would often invite intellectuals who were far from faithfully Catholic to present papers at his annual Catholic Bioethics conference. This would result in a flurry of phone calls to my office from people wanting to know which side Nick was really on and I quickly learned to take my annual leave in the pre-conference period.

Toward the end of his life, Nicholas did start to appreciate the persuasive power of beauty. He started to understand that people are sometimes converted to a Catholic way of looking at the world, not through dialectical rationality, but through the beauty of the truth. He became a convert to the idea that beauty is very important for the work of evangelization. He enjoyed our lunch time conversations about beauty because he thought it gave him a window into the intellectual world of his two daughters, especially Lucianne, who wrote her Masters dissertation on the philosophy of the fashion industry.

In class, however, beauty was not high on Nick's list of priorities. Nick's classes were the academic equivalent of SAS training camps in the sense of the level of intellectual rigor that was expected. He was particularly fond of scheduling class debates on controversial topics. The debates were often quite comical as people who had taken religious vows stood up to deliver a passionate defense of some atheistic position. After I declared the pro-euthanasia team to be the winners for three years in a row, he said to me, in his deep, stern voice, "Tracey, you had better hope that *The Age* [the local secular and decidedly anti-Catholic newspaper] doesn't hear about this!"

Towards the end of his life, he would tell students that they shouldn't be ashamed to own their Christianity in the public domain. In his own experience he found that people were much more comfortable with him when he freely acknowledged that he was operating within a Judeo-Christian framework. He thought it was disingenuous for Catholic intellectuals to stand up in public and say that their positions were founded on nothing but "pure reason."

Earlier in his public intellectual life, he had tried to argue a "pure reason" position, thinking that his interlocutors would reject anything that was faith-related, but he came to the conclusion that everyone has some kind of faith, some underlying presumption that cannot be scientifically proven, and he found that people got along a whole lot better on committees when they were allowed to bring their faith to the table, rather than pretending not to have any.

This is not to say that he thought that in the public domain one can simply assert something to be true because the Catholic Church claims that it is. But he did think it was quite acceptable to publicly acknowledge that his belief in the sacrality of human life was tied to his faith in Christ.

Nicholas also came to the conclusion that among the younger generations of Catholics there was a pastoral crisis created by their lack of understanding of sacramentality. He came to understand that if you spend twelve years teaching school children all the rationalistic reasons why they should be good, it is not surprising that when they are in the late teens and early 20s they don't understand the moral difference between cohabitation and a sacramental marriage. They need at least a rudimentary acquaintance with Trinitarian theology and the concept of grace if they are to understand the difference. In the final years of his life he therefore focused on strengthening the bridge between sacramental theology and moral theology.

As his health continued to decline he would often work to keep his mind off the pain and he developed the habit of sending out long emails while he was on dialysis. These emails were never malicious, but they were somewhat acutely blunt. I think he would use the time when he was on dialysis to think of all the things that his fellow faculty members could do if there were 50 hours in every day instead of 24, and then let us know in case he didn't survive the dialysis session. We would have a record of what he thought needed to be done, by whom, and why.

Of all the faculty members, I was the one who worked most closely with Nicholas over a fourteen-year period. I have lost count of the number of bureaucratic battles that we fought together and I think I can say from experience that when it comes to trench warfare, there was none braver than Nicholas. I will miss his chivalry and his sense of humor. He was born to be a general but he so often found himself serving in the ecclesial equivalent of Dad's Army.

I recently read this description of the personality of John Henry Newman and it reminded me very much of Nicholas:

> Newman could not abide the philistine, the creature coarse in morals and feeling, and dull in mind and spirit. He could not comprehend the bourgeois mind, the enemy of light and the children of light. His spirit was hierarchical and aristocratic in the finest way, that is, he was anti-mediocre, hostile not to the people but to mob-judgments and mob-standards, hostile to complacency.

Eulogy for Professor Nicholas Tonti-Filippini

I was delighted when in 2009 Pope Benedict made Nicholas a Knight of St. Gregory. He received that honor, not because he had donated a million dollars to some papal charity, but because he had over several decades heroically defended the Catholic faith in the public sphere. He was a model of how to use one's intellect in the service of Christ and his Church.

When he was younger and still able to travel to Rome, Cardinal Ratzinger would invite him to his office in the Congregation for the Doctrine of the Faith for coffee and Bavarian cake and a chat about the theological issues of the day. He was able to move with ease in these exalted ecclesial circles.

These facts notwithstanding, he was never what one might call a Captain Catholic type. He was never sycophantic around members of the clergy. He wasn't a nerd desperate to be noticed by bishops and he wasn't a self-promoter. He could also be quite mischievous in the presence of dignitaries. When the Papal Nuncio recently visited the Institute and asked the predictable question "what are your current projects," Nicholas not only informed him of the conference on Fertility Awareness but offered the Nuncio a medical textbook account of the differences between the three most popular methods of discerning when a woman is fertile. That Nuncio has now been promoted to a very senior position in the Vatican and I don't know how Nick's information could ever be of any practical value to him, but he will certainly never forget his morning at the JPII Institute in Melbourne. It was not just another morning shaking hands and making polite small talk.

Nicholas was also interested in the ideas of people outside the Church. One of those was the French philosopher and mystic, Simone Weil, who never became a Catholic but was a believing Christian. In an essay on "The Love of God and Affliction," Weil wrote:

As for us [humans], our misery gives us the infinitely precious privilege of sharing in the distance placed between God the Son and God the Father.... For those who love, separation, although painful, is a good, because it is love. Even the distress of the abandoned Christ is a good [and] there cannot be a greater good for us on earth than to share in it.

God can never be perfectly present to us here below on account of our flesh.... [However] a day comes when the soul belongs to God, when it not only consents to love but when truly and effectively it loves. Then ... it must cross the universe to go to God.... It is for this crossing to God that we are created and this alone.[1]

I think that Nicholas would like that quotation. Its truth is something he lived on a daily basis. He knew the pain of the cross, but the pain helped him to love.

If there is a computer center in heaven, I am sure that Nicholas will find it. But instead of emailing us, there will be angels in various departments receiving messages about what Mary needs, what Justin, John, Lucianne, Claire, and James need and what various students and faculty of the Institute need, what Lieutenant-Colonel Toby Hunter needs, what Joan Clements and the Billings teachers need, what his friend Archbishop Fisher needs. Any sleepy angel who fails to respond quickly will find himself demoted to a lower rank in the choir of angels and put on duty guarding Bishop Elliott's cat.

---

[1] Simone Weil, *Waiting on God* (Glasgow: Collins, 1977), 86.

18

The Doctrinal Mission of
St Thérèse of Lisieux

MY FIRST ENCOUNTER WITH ST
Thérèse of Lisieux was seeing the standard image
of a young Carmelite holding a bunch of roses and a
crucifix in her arms in the dining room of the convent attached
to my primary school. One of the nuns explained to me that
it was an image of St Thérèse of Lisieux, known as the "Little
Flower." At that time she was one of the two patron saints of
Australia (the second was St Francis Xavier), declared such
at a time when Australia was considered a mission country
without any home-grown saints of its own. In 1976 Australia
graduated from the class of mission countries, and St Thérèse
and St Francis Xavier's patronage responsibilities have since
officially been taken over by St Mary MacKillop, but I like to
think that St Thérèse has not lost interest in what the Spanish
called "the land of the Holy Spirit." I also like to imagine that she
takes a special interest in the parish of St Patrick's, Soho, since
it seems to serve as the Australian Catholic embassy in London.

In 1997 St Thérèse was declared a doctor of the Church by
St John Paul II, joining fellow Carmelites St John of the Cross
and St Teresa of Avila. At the time this struck many commen-
tators as an odd decision. It seemed that the more obvious
choice for a contemporary Carmelite Church Doctor was Edith
Stein — known by her religious name St Teresa Benedicta of
the Cross — who was a highly distinguished scholar before
her martyrdom in the Auschwitz concentration camp. St John

---

*Lecture delivered in St Patrick's Church, Soho, London, November
2017, to raise money for a stained-glass window of St Thérèse.*

Paul II did declare Edith Stein one of the six patron saints of Europe, the others being St Augustine, St Benedict, Sts Cyril and Methodius, St Bridget of Sweden and St Catherine of Siena, but it was to Thérèse he awarded the more "academic" honor. To understand why he did so, we need to begin with *Divini Amoris Scientia*, the Apostolic Letter proclaiming St Thérèse a Doctor of the Church. In this we find the following statements from St. John Paul II:

> Thérèse of the Child Jesus left us writings that deservedly qualify her as a teacher of the spiritual life. Her principal work remains the account of her life in three autobiographical manuscripts (*Manuscrits autobiographiques* A, B, C), first published with the soon to be famous title of *Histoire d'une Âme*.... In these three different manuscripts, which converge in a thematic unity and in a progressive description of her life and spiritual way, Thérèse has left us an original autobiography which is the story of her soul. It shows how in her life God has offered the world a precise message, indicating an evangelical way, the "little way," which everyone can take, because everyone is called to holiness.
>
> In the 266 letters we possess, addressed to family members, women religious and missionary "brothers," Thérèse shares her wisdom, developing a teaching that is actually a profound exercise in the spiritual direction of souls.

John Paul II concluded that one can find in this small literary output her "eminent doctrine." He describes the "core of her message" as "the mystery of God-Love, of the Triune God, infinitely perfect in himself." As he explains:

At the summit, as the source and goal, is the merciful love of the three Divine persons, as she expresses it, especially in her Act of Oblation to Merciful Love. At the root, on the subject's part, is the experience of being the father's adoptive children in Jesus; this is the most authentic meaning of spiritual childhood, that is, the experience of divine filiation, under the movement of the Holy Spirit. At the root again, and standing before us, is our neighbor, others, for whose salvation we must collaborate with and in Jesus, with the same merciful love as his.

Through spiritual childhood one experiences that everything comes from God, returns to him and abides in him, for the salvation of all, in a mystery of merciful love. Such is the doctrinal message taught and lived by this Saint.

Echoing the first sentence of his first encyclical, *Redemptor Hominis*, in presenting Jesus Christ, the redeemer of man, as the center and purpose of human history, John Paul II noted that "in her spiritual experience Christ is the center and fullness of Revelation." In other words, the Incarnation is the fulcrum around which the rest of human history turns. This was one of the key theological motifs of the papacy of John Paul II.

Finally, John Paul II called attention to the fact that St Thérèse received particular light on the reality of Christ's mystical Body, on the variety of charisms in the life of the Church, on the many gifts of the Holy Spirit, and on the eminent power of love. He concluded: "among the most original chapters of her spiritual doctrine, we must recall Thérèse's wise delving into the mystery and journey of the Virgin Mary, achieving results very close to the doctrine of the Second Vatican Council in chapter eight of the Constitution *Lumen Gentium* and to what [he himself] taught in the Encyclical Letter *Redemptoris Mater* of 1987." Explicit references to St Thérèse's teaching can also be found inserted into the *Catechism of the Catholic Church*, at paragraphs 127, 826, 956, 1011, 2011, and 2558.

The emphasis within the Apostolic Letter on the idea of the merciful love of God, expressed most bountifully to those who approach the throne of mercy with the disposition of trusting children, is evocative of the divine mercy spirituality associated with Poland's St Faustina, who exercised such a strong influence on John Paul II that he instituted the Feast of Divine Mercy as an endorsement of her spiritual mission.

In an essay discussing the links between the missions of the two saints, Fr Angelo Casimiro of the Franciscan University of Steubenville wrote:

> In her *Diary*, St. Faustina related how, as a novice, she was going through some difficulties that she did not know how to overcome. She started a novena to St. Thérèse of the Child Jesus since she had a great devotion to her. On the fifth day of the novena, St. Faustina dreamed of St. Thérèse. The Little Flower told her not to be worried about the matter but that she should *trust* more in God. At first, St. Thérèse hid the fact that she [Faustina] was a saint. She said that she suffered greatly, too, but St. Faustina did not quite believe her. The Little Flower assured her that she had suffered very much, indeed, and told St. Faustina that in three days the difficulty she was having would come to a happy conclusion. At that moment, St. Thérèse revealed to her that she was a saint. Saint Faustina then asked her if she was going to go to heaven and become a saint — one raised to the altar like her. The Little Flower assured St. Faustina

that she would become a saint like her but that she must *trust* in the Lord Jesus.[1]

I will leave it for some future doctoral student to write a dissertation on the topic of whether the two saints each shared the same spiritual mission, or whether their missions were similar in many ways but nuanced differently. Certainly they both anticipated the emphasis at the Second Vatican Council on the universal call to holiness and the place of merciful love and childlike openness to this love in the quest for holiness. St Thérèse distinguished her doctrine from those of other guides to the spiritual life by saying that, unlike those who laid out a strategic plan for holiness consisting of various practices and mortifications, Thérèse searched for what she called an "elevator" that would get her up to the heights of holiness without first floundering about on the various floors below the top story. For Thérèse, a disposition of childlike trust in God's merciful love was the elevator.

The great French Oratorian Louis Bouyer (1913–2004) had this to say of the so-called "Little Way" or elevator:

> The Thérèsian "little way" is simply the logic of St. Paul's justification by faith, understood as Saint Thomas Aquinas himself understood it: that is, a justification by faith alone, not in that heretical sense into which Luther, enraged by an uncomprehending polemic, was to fall: as if man had nothing more to do, could remain just as he is since he has faith, but indeed in the sense given by Saint Paul himself: "I can do all things through him who strengthens me," responding in a way to the affirmation of the Savior

1 Angelo Casimiro, "Spiritual Childhood: How Thérèse and Faustina Blazed a Trail of Holiness," www.marian.org/divinemercy/story.php?NID.

himself, transmitted by Saint John: "Outside of me, you can do nothing!"[2]

Bouyer goes on to say: "This will explain why Thérèse has been able to convert Protestants, like that Pastor Grant, of the Presbyterian Church of Scotland, who had a vision of her and whose widow... was until her death the caretaker of the house in which Thérèse was born, in Alençon."[3] It also perhaps explains the popularity of St. Thérèse among soldiers caught in the trenches of the Somme in World War I, among whom many were Protestants.

Bouyer concludes that the principal rediscovery of St Thérèse for the Church of our times is that the entire gospel of Jesus is the gospel of the Father, and thus that we Catholics exist in a filial relationship with God the Father, a theological point underscored by John Paul II in his encyclical *Dives in Misericordia* (1980).[4] In the first paragraph of this encyclical John Paul II stated:

> The more the Church's mission is centered upon man — the more it is, so to speak, anthropocentric — the more it must be confirmed and actualized theo-centrically, that is to say, be directed in Jesus Christ to the Father. While the various currents of human thought both in the past and at the present have tended and still tend to separate theo-centrism and anthropocentrism, and even to set them in opposition to each other, the Church, following Christ, seeks to link them up in human history, in a deep and organic way.

To put this point more simply, it is impossible to understand the human person without first understanding his or her

2 Louis Bouyer, *Women Mystics* (San Francisco: Ignatius, 1993), 147–48.
3 Ibid., 148.
4 Ibid., 154.

relationship with God the Father, God the Son, and God the Holy Spirit. Any adequate anthropology must be theological. If we turn now to Hans Urs von Balthasar (1905–88), the great Swiss theologian and mentor of Joseph Ratzinger/Benedict XVI, we find the following judgement:

> Every Christian—and, much more, every saint—lives theological truths: his life is an expression of the Gospel teaching whose kernel is found in the unity of truth and life. [But] Thérèse's mission goes beyond this; it is, in the Pope's words, an explicitly doctrinal mission. It was God's purpose for Thérèse to light up certain aspects of revelation afresh for the benefit of contemporary Christendom, to make certain neglected truths astonishingly clear. She herself was aware of this doctrinal mission and she does not hesitate to underline its significance.[5]

Balthasar goes onto to say that St Thérèse's teaching is "not a theological system of propositions held together by inferences; it is an immediate, total vision" about the centrality of love in the Mystical Body.[6] He further suggests that Thérèse is a warrior whose "battle is to wipe out the hard core of Pharisaism which persists in the midst of Christianity; that will-to-power disguised in the mantle of religion."[7]

Thérèse liked military metaphors as well as horticultural metaphors, not just roses and violets and daisies but soldiers and battles. She told novices to behave like brave soldiers who don't complain about their own sufferings but focus on the

5 Hans Urs von Balthasar, *Two Sisters in the Spirit: Thérèse of Lisieux and Elizabeth of the Trinity* (San Francisco: Ignatius, 1998), 233.
6 Ibid., 237.
7 Ibid., 241.

wounds of others while treating their own as mere scratches. She revered St Joan of Arc and identified with her, but stated that she "realized that [her] mission was not to get a mortal king crowned but to get the King of Heaven loved, to bring the realm of hearts under His sway."[8]

Balthasar also drew attention to the importance of two aspects of the Trinity that are manifest in Thérèse's teaching: the Son incarnate, "the suffering Son who invites man to co-operate in his work and to whom we can offer all our love; and then the Father, but not so much the Father in his Trinitarian relations with the Son and the Holy Spirit, as the Father who represents divine goodness and mercy, and in whose arms we can nestle."[9]

Anna Silvas, the author of several works on Church Doctors, including St Basil the Great and St Hildegard of Bingen, has further suggested that in terms of the genealogy of ideas and the deeper structures of what is happening in society, Thérèse's particular vocation is significant in two ways:

1. Thérèse's "rediscovery" (as it were) of God's merciful love was a providential antidote to the toxic cramping of the spirit that came of the Jansenist influence on the French church in particular and the broader Western church in general.
2. There is surely some mysterious link between Thérèse and the demonic nihilism of Nietzsche in the last decade of his life, the 1890s. It is as if she is in some sense God's answer to this self-destructive nihilism, almost its exorcism, through her experience of profound union with Christ crucified, a union shot through with a hidden and sublime fruitfulness through deifying charity.

8 Ibid., 240.
9 Ibid., 300.

Jansenism was a theological movement that emphasized original sin, human depravity, and predestination. The movement originated from the posthumously published work of the Dutch theologian Cornelius Jansen, who died in 1638. It was particularly strong in France, and in the post-revolutionary era when clergy were leaving France for more Catholic-friendly countries the theological virus spread with them. Jansenists are often described as Catholic Calvinists. Two of their hallmarks are a Puritan attitude toward sexuality and a corresponding opposition to sensual and thus high liturgy. It is often said that John Paul II's *Catechesis on Human Love* was the much-needed antidote to Jansenist ideas about sexuality.

In the Church in France, a counterweight to the Jansenist influence was the spirituality of St Francis de Sales (1567–1622), who had been tortured in his youth by thoughts of predestination and of never being worthy of God. It was a baleful effect of the strict Calvinist doctrine then besieging his native region of Savoy. He overcame his own spiritual crisis through a conversion to a deep sense of God's all-enveloping love and benevolence and will to save. The spirituality of St Francis de Sales, along with St Margaret Mary Alocoque's (1647–90) mission of spreading devotion to the Sacred Heart, were significant precursors to the doctrinal mission of St Thérèse.

Combing through the academic literature, one can also find several papers dedicated to the theme of Thérèse as God's answer to Friedrich Nietzsche, the 19th-century German philosopher who declared that "God is dead." Nietzsche was brought up in a Protestant family surrounded by maiden aunts who were not much fun. As an adult he went to war against Christianity, describing it as a crime against life itself and the morality of the herd. His books were a source of inspiration for the generation of 1968. Fr Dwight Longenecker has contrasted the mentalities of Thérèse and Nietzsche in the following passage:

If Friedrich Nietzsche met Thérèse Martin how would the conversation go? He might explain the death of God and the inexorable rise of nihilism. Thérèse would say "the good God" was not dead, but only man's false ideas of God had died. When he explained how morality was discovered by each person Thérèse would reply that each person did indeed have to discover morality—but discover the reality of the received morality in a radically personal way. When Nietzsche explained how the great ones had to give up fitting into dull society, had to give up attachment to all material things, Thérèse would agree and point out that this is precisely what she aimed to do by becoming a Carmelite. When Nietzsche explained that this process of negation and discovery of true values was the process by which the superman came to be, Thérèse would agree, but she would call that superman a saint. When she cries, "Sanctity! It must be won at the point of a sword!" or "You cannot be half a saint. You must be a whole saint or no saint at all," she gives the world her own version of the superman—one who has overcome the dull conventional beliefs and behaviors and risen to another dimension of humanity altogether.[10]

Not only is St Thérèse an anti-Nietzschean figure, a showcase example of the humanism of the Incarnation contrasted with the radically secular humanism of Nietzsche and his followers, but her own spiritual trials, which included having to believe without any sense of spiritual consolation—to go on

10   Fr Dwight Longenecker, "Thérèse or Nietzsche: It's All or Nuthin," https://theimaginativeconservative.org/2015/05/therese-or-nietzsche-its-all-or-nuthin.html.

believing and trusting in utter spiritual darkness — foreshadow the spiritual challenge of many Catholics in the contemporary world who find little within the Church or the world that is inspirational and consoling.

This modern spiritual predicament was the subject of a number of poems by the Australian author James McAuley (1917–76), who grew up in a Protestant family in Sydney and was converted to the Catholic faith when working as a foreign-affairs official in Papua New Guinea. Here he had the good fortune to develop a friendship with the Archbishop of Port Moresby, Alain de Boismenu, a French Missionary of the Sacred Heart and friend of the poet Paul Claudel. McAuley was to describe de Boismenu (whose cause for beatification is currently before the Congregation for the Saints) as a man with the heart of a lion.

In McAuley's *Captain Quiros* — his poem about the quest of Captain Pedro Fernandez de Quiros to settle Australia in the name of the Spanish crown and thereby ensure that Australia would not fall into the hands of the Protestant British — McAuley speaks of the differences between the era of Christendom and our own modern era. Those who live within the culture of Modernity he describes as "Children of the Second Syllable" — the first syllable being "Christ," the second "tus" (in the name "Christus"). "Tus," he tells us, means incense (*thus* in Latin), a substance we burn to purify.

In that section of the poem entitled "The Last Vision," he writes:

> The architecture of the world we knew,
> The cosmic temple framed with cross and dome,
> And circle, square and column, proportioned true,
> Lies empty like a ruined honeycomb.
> For colder, vaster systems rise instead;

Beyond this earth discovery lies ahead,
But nowhere can man's spirit find a home.

And now within that Ocean hemisphere
Where fabled monsters lurked until our ships
Dispersed old fancies, dreadful signs appear,
Figures and portents of apocalypse.
The ancient Dragon wakes and knows his hour...

I heard a voice cry as deep twilight falls,
Speaking to men in vision: "You shall be
The children of the second syllable,"
And by that word they know their destiny
In the name of Christus the first sound means chrism —
The creature hallowed after exorcism;
The second sound means incense literally.

These signify two ages. In the first,
From pagan rubble Christendom was built;
But in it the first One still cried: I thirst.
So, for God's greater plan and for our guilt,
Altars and thrones are toppled and destroyed
The christened castellated realms laid void,
Till grace and nature both appear to wilt.

Now in a time of loneliness and death
The just shall live by faith without the aid
Of custom that bound man to heaven and earth
Estranged within the city man has made,
Like smoke of sacrifice they shall arise,
Or vapour drawn up swiftly to the skies,
Unknown or counted as of little worth.

In this vision, contemporary Christians are more than the salt of the earth, more than that which gives a culture its flavor. They are, he suggests, self-sacrificial offerings. Their heroism consists in maintaining fidelity to Christ in circumstances where all the social benefits which may once have flowed from this have been destroyed. Nonetheless, McAuley goes on to write that in the lives of these children of the second syllable, "time's fullness has begun." Such lives give "fresh impulse to men's failing arts." They "take the world from which they seemed estranged into love's workshop where it will be changed, though they themselves die wretched and alone."

The reference here is to a kind of white martyrdom — the gift of human life as incense — a sacrifice of love which differs from the days of being fed to lions for popular entertainment. This is a deeply Carmelite spirituality.

The theme of the necessity of self-sacrificial love to sustain the practices of Christianity is especially strong in McAuley's *Celebration of Divine Love*, which could be read as an ode to St Thérèse. It ends with the words:

> You gentle souls who sit contemplative
> In the walled garden where the fountain flows,
> And faint with longing have desire to live
> But the brief flowering of the single rose,
> Knowing that all you give
> Into the keeping of your tender Lord
> Shall be enriched and thousandfold restored:
> Before the herons return
> Abide the sharp frosts and the time of pruning;
> For he shall come at last for whom you yearn
>
> And deep and silent shall be your communing
> And if his summer heat of love should burn

Its victim with a sacrificial fire,
Rejoice: who knows what wanderer may turn,
Responsive to that fragrant hidden pyre!

With reference to St Thérèse's experience of this sacrificial fire, Anna Silvas has suggested that there is an interesting parallel between the spiritual trials of St Thérèse of Lisieux and those of St Teresa of Calcutta. Just as St Thérèse experienced a terrible spiritual darkness in the last year and a half of her brief life, so too St Teresa of Calcutta experienced a terrible spiritual darkness for decades of her much-longer life. According to Silvas, the darkness experienced by these two holy women was not necessarily that of the Night of the Spirit as described by St John of the Cross, but something supererogatory to their own spiritual progress. It had in effect a certain vicarious quality on behalf of others.

The following passage, taken from St. Thérèse's autobiography, appears in the Liturgy of the Hours for her feast day on October 1. It offers a sketch of her own self-understanding of her mission:

> Since my longing for martyrdom was powerful and
> unsettling, I turned to the epistles of St Paul in the
> hope of finally finding an answer. By chance the 12th
> and 13th chapters of the 1st Epistle to the Corinthians
> caught my attention, and in the first section I read that
> not everyone can be an apostle, prophet or teacher,
> that the Church is composed of a variety of members,
> and that the eye cannot be the hand. Even with such
> an answer revealed before me, I was unsatisfied, and
> did not find peace.
>
> I persevered in reading and did not let my mind
> wander until I found this encouraging theme: *Set your*

*desires on the higher gifts. And I am going to show you
a way which surpasses all the others.* For the Apostle
insists that without love the greater gifts are nothing at
all, and that this same love is surely the best path leading directly to God. Finally I had found peace of soul.
When I looked upon the mystical body of the
Church, I recognized myself in none of the members
which St Paul described, and what is more, I desired
to distinguish myself more favorably within the whole
body. Love appeared to me to be the hinge for my
vocation. Indeed I knew that the Church had a body
composed of various members, but in this body the
necessary and more noble member was not lacking;
I knew that the Church had a heart and that such a
heart appeared to be aflame with love. I knew that one
love drove the members of the Church to action, and
that if this love were extinguished, the apostle would
have proclaimed the Gospel no longer, the martyrs
have shed their blood no more. I saw and realized that
love sets off the bounds of all vocations, that love is
everything, that this same love embraces every time
and every place. In one word, love is everlasting.

Then, nearly ecstatic with the supreme joy of my
soul, I proclaimed: O Jesus, my love, at last I have
found my calling: my call is love. Surely I have found
my place in the Church, and you have given me that
place, my God. In the heart of the Church, my mother,
I will be love, and thus I will be all things, as my desire
finds its direction.

In Thérèse, then, this Doctor of the Church who died at
only 24 years of age, we can say that for all the poverty (in
strictly academic terms) of her theological formation, here

was an *intellect* intimately open to the effects of the Holy Spirit. Through her deliberate habitual cleaving to God in faith and love and hope, she was able to say things that at times far transcended the product of mere learned discourse.

19

James V. Schall, SJ:
Uncle, Father, Jesuit, Professor, Giant

THE MARKETING BLURB ON THE BOOK *When Jesuits Were Giants* begins with the statement: "No one in France or the United States during the second half of the nineteenth century doubted that the Jesuits, loved and honored by friends, hated and feared by enemies, were a force to be reckoned with. Scholars, missionaries, educators, adventurers, social innovators — they were Renaissance men, giants."

This Holy Week the Church has lost one of the last sons of St. Ignatius in this mould.

"Uncle Jim" to his vast extended family, Fr Jim to his friends, and Professor James V. Schall, SJ, to generations of political philosophy students, passed away at 12:48 PDT on Wednesday, April 17th, 2019.

He has been described as "America's Chesterton" because of the style and humor of his opinion-piece reflections on contemporary ecclesial and social life. He was also a world-class political philosopher. He not only knew what St Augustine or St Thomas Aquinas had said about some political issue, he could go through the entire Western canon, starting with the pre-Socratics and working his way through the Church Fathers and the medievals, until he finally reached the moderns. The post-moderns he thought were just mad and not worthy of his attention: anyone who thinks that 2 + 2 might in some alternative universe equal 5 had some kind of mental disability.

As is typical of these Renaissance types, he was open to all that classical wisdom had to offer, but argued that there were

Published in The Catholic World Report, *April 18, 2019.*

certain problems beyond the capacities of even the greatest of the Greeks and Romans to solve. These hitherto unresolved issues required the Incarnation — a kind of ontological revolution. Educated people had to be at least open to the possibility that this really did happen, that God really did become incarnate in human form, since it is the only way of making sense of "all that is" (one of his favorite phrases).

It is said that students would enroll at Georgetown University just to "Major in Schall." In a sense, he was his own academic department.

I first came across his name when I was an undergraduate in the 1980s. Instead of reading the books my lecturers had recommended, I would spend hours in the library working my way through articles by James V. Schall.

On my first trip to the States in 1988 I found my way to Fr Jim's office at Georgetown. I was in my early 20s and it never occurred to me to send a polite letter before I turned up outside his door. I simply tracked him down and introduced myself as someone who loved his work. He was about to go and deliver a lecture but he told me he would talk to me after the class. I asked if I could stay in his office and look at his library, and he agreed to that. I spent a couple of hours taking down references to books on his shelves, and when he reappeared he gave me a cup of tea, we had an academic chat, and then he took me on a tour of his University. I can't remember anything about our intellectual exchange but I do remember his walking up to students who were smoking and praising them for having the courage to be politically incorrect. Their responses indicated that they knew who he was and that they loved him.

Quite simply he had the capacity to be an intellectual father to many because he was himself a very together alpha male who knew perfectly well that $2 + 2 = 4$.

Not only did he not like political correctness, he had an especially mordant view of feminism. This did not mean he thought women in any sense inferior to men. He had many friendships with intellectual women and was proud of the females he had taught who went on to occupy high professional positions. Those in this category included Janne Haaland Matláry, a Professor of International Relations at the University of Oslo, who served as Norway's State Secretary in the Ministry of Foreign Affairs from 1997 to 2000. However, he thought that women who wanted to be like men, who didn't value their femininity, or who thought that marriage and family life was somehow beneath them, were victims of an ideology. He also thought that men and women were "wired differently," and he was the chivalrous, dragon-slaying type who preferred to put women on a pedestal and worship them, rather than virtue-signalling his belief in gender equality.

When I first arrived at Cambridge University, he would send me copies of his publications in envelopes addressed to "Mrs Stuart Rowland." This really impressed the porters at my college who were mostly former military men. They were not much into feminism either. A memo actually went around the porter's lodge to the effect that all post arriving to "Mrs Stuart Rowland" was to be put in Tracey Rowland's pigeon-hole, since when Fr Schall's envelopes first started arriving, no one knew what to do with them. I was later told by the college chaplain that I was one of the porter's favorite students and I think it was because they loved this little act of politically incorrect chutzpah.

Before I went to Cambridge, and when I was a complete academic nobody, I managed to publish an opinion piece about post-modern philosophy in a secular newspaper. Fr Jim liked it and used a quotation from it in one of his articles, citing "Tracey Rowland" alongside Aristotle and St. Augustine. He then sent me the article with a short covering note saying "Happy

St. Valentine's Day — regards to Stuart, pray for me, Fr Jim!" I made multiple photocopies of his article and proudly handed out copies to my friends. One of them joked that I was lucky to be mentioned alongside Aristotle and Augustine and not Snoopy and Schroeder. He loved the Peanuts cartoons!

However, by far his greatest act of chivalry occurred when my book *Ratzinger's Faith* received a two-page "bad review" in the *Times Literary Supplement*. *Ratzinger's Faith* actually sold very well and was translated into three other languages, and my publisher was not at all concerned about the fact that the reviewer didn't like my book. The publisher said: "a double-page spread in the TLS is a double-page spread in the TLS" — in other words, all publicity is good publicity. The reviewer, however, had ridiculed my book by calling it "a papal romance." He said words to the effect that I was in love with Ratzinger, and that my reading was completely unreliable because it didn't square with the profile of Ratzinger that he had been given in his interviews with Hans Küng.

What annoyed me most about the review was that my book was not a biography in the sense of an attempt to deal with Ratzinger the man, but only with his ideas. Even theological liberals agree with me that Ratzinger was never a liberal, which is one of the points I tried to emphasize.

In any event, when news of the "papal romance" article reached Fr Jim via his friend Monsignor Sokolowski, he was in hospital recovering from an operation for cancer of the mouth. At the time he was being fed through a drip but he still managed to type out an article blasting the reviewer for all manner of intellectual ineptitudes. The reviewer informed Fr Jim that he had friends in the Society of Jesus. Fr Jim's response was something along the lines of "so what, I am 80-something, in hospital, with cancer, do your worst."

No doubt many academic articles will be written in the

years ahead about Fr Jim's contribution to Catholic political philosophy. His books and papers will be his legacy to future generations. Unlike so many other Jesuits since the Arrupe era, he never went down the path of fostering the rag-bag of Leftist political causes. He had no time whatsoever for Marxism. He believed that there will always be elites and that the best thing a Jesuit could do would be to ensure that the elites were in both belief and practice *Catholic*. He thought that if the social leaders were good, holy people, then this would foster the good of all. The idea of allowing Communists a say in the choice of bishops was, for him, an idea from planet Pluto, or maybe even from hell.

When new generations of Catholic students want to study political philosophy, the name "Schall" will feature prominently on their book lists. Already his book *Another Sort of Learning* is well known in Catholic undergraduate circles. It offers extensive reading lists for students who want to immerse themselves in the Catholic intellectual tradition.

For those of us who knew him, who were privileged to be on his mailing list, there is a sense that we haven't just lost a friend, we have lost one of the last old-style renaissance-men of the Jesuits. We have lost one of the giants!

20

The Benedictine Roots of Western Civilization

I N HIS GENERAL AUDIENCE HOMILY DELIV-
ered on the 9th of April in 2008, Pope Benedict referred
his listeners to St Gregory the Great's work simply called
Dialogues for information on the life and holiness of St Benedict.
Pope Benedict wrote:

> This perspective of the "biographer" [Pope St Gregory
> the Great] is also explained in light of the general con-
> text of his time: straddling the fifth and sixth centuries,
> "the world was overturned by a tremendous crisis of
> values and institutions caused by the collapse of the
> Roman Empire, the invasion of new peoples and the
> decay of morals." But in this terrible situation, here, in
> this very city of Rome, Gregory presented St Benedict
> as a "luminous star" in order to point the way out of
> the "black night of history" (cf. John Paul II, 18 May
> 1979). In fact, the Saint's work and particularly his *Rule*
> were to prove heralds of an authentic spiritual leaven
> which, in the course of the centuries, far beyond the
> boundaries of his country and [his] time, changed
> the face of Europe following the fall of the political
> unity created by the Roman Empire, inspiring a new
> spiritual and cultural unity, that of the Christian faith
> shared by the peoples of the Continent. This is how
> the reality we call "Europe" came into being.

---

*Address delivered at St Benedict's Parish, Broadway, Sydney, on July 26,
2018 to celebrate the 180th anniversary of the foundation of the Parish.*

Today St Benedict of Nursia is venerated as a Patron Saint of Europe, along with Sts Cyril and Methodius, who are known as the apostles to the Slavs, St Edith Stein, St Bridget of Sweden, and St Catherine of Siena.

St Benedict founded twelve communities for monks at Subiaco in Italy, which is 64 km east of Rome, before moving to Monte Cassino, a rocky hill about 130 km southeast of Rome.

Today Monte Cassino is also associated with one of the bloodiest battles in World War II. It is said that the battle claimed some 200,000 casualties on both sides. The mountain lay in a strategic location along the road to Rome. In the end the allies did capture it, largely thanks to Polish and British troops. The Poles lost 923 men in the fighting and the Polish cemetery at Monte Cassino is today a major site for Polish pilgrims. In many Polish cities one finds avenues dedicated to the Bohaterów Monte Cassino (the Heroes of Monte Cassino) and there is a monument to the heroes near the gates of the Krasiński Gardens in Warsaw.

According to St Gregory the Great, the monastery of Monte Cassino was founded on an older pagan site where there existed a temple dedicated to the god Apollo. St Benedict is recorded as having smashed the sculpture of Apollo and destroyed the altar dedicated to him. In place of the temple he built a Christian church with chapels dedicated to Saint Martin of Tours (who incidentally was Hungarian, not French) and Saint John the Baptist.

Pope Gregory's account of Benedict's seizure of Monte Cassino is as follows:

> Now the citadel called Casinum is located on the side of a high mountain. The mountain shelters this citadel on a broad bench. Then it rises three miles above it as if its peak tended toward heaven. There was an ancient temple there in which Apollo used

to be worshipped according to the old pagan rite by the foolish local farmers. Around it had grown up a grove dedicated to demon worship, where even at that time a wild crowd still devoted themselves to unholy sacrifices. When [Benedict] the man of God arrived, he smashed the idol, overturned the altar and cut down the grove of trees. He built a chapel dedicated to St. Martin in the temple of Apollo and another to St. John where the altar of Apollo had stood. And he summoned the people of the district to the faith by his unceasing preaching.

Pope Gregory goes on to say that Satan opposed the demolition of the pagan temple and was often interfering in Benedict's building projects, but Benedict was able to perform miracles to out-fox Satan.

Today, St Benedict is called the founder of Western monasticism, and his *Rule* or precepts for governing a monastery and fostering sanctity among the brethren is the basis for many religious communities. It is acknowledged that some of his ideas came from John Cassian (c. 360–c. 435), a monk who lived a century earlier than Benedict who was influenced by the spirituality of the Desert Fathers of Egypt.

One of the principles of the *Rule* is that the monks devote eight hours a day to prayer, eight hours to sleep and eight hours to manual work, sacred reading, or works of charity.

In the 19th century Blessed John Henry Newman wrote:

The panegyrists of this illustrious Order [that is, the religious communities which derive their *Rule* from St Benedict] are accustomed to claim for it in all its branches as many as 37,000 houses, and, besides, 30 Popes, 200 Cardinals, 4 Emperors, 46 Kings, 51 Queens,

1,406 Princes, 1,600 Archbishops, 600 Bishops, 2,400 Nobles, and 15,000 Abbots and learned men.[1]

Newman went on to write:

Nor are the religious bodies which sprang from St. Benedict the full measure of what he has accomplished.... His *Rule* gradually made its way into those various monasteries which were of an earlier or of an independent foundation. It first coalesced with, and then supplanted, the Irish Rule of St. Columban in France, and the still older institutes which had been brought from the East by St. Athanasius, St. Eusebius, and St. Martin. At the beginning of the ninth century it was formally adopted throughout the dominions of Charlemagne. Pure, or with some admixture, it was brought by St. Augustine [of Canterbury] to England; and that admixture, if it existed, was gradually eliminated by St. Wilfrid, St. Dunstan, and Lanfranc, till at length it was received, with the name and obedience of St. Benedict, in all the Cathedral monasteries (to mention no others), excepting Carlisle. Nor did it cost such regular bodies any very great effort to make the change, even when historically most separate from St. Benedict; for the Saint had taken up for the most part what he found, and his *Rule* was but the expression of the genius of monachism in those first times of the Church, with a more exact adaptation to their needs than could elsewhere be met with.

The English Catholic historian Christopher Dawson has

---

[1] John Henry Newman, "The Mission of St. Benedict," *Atlantis*, January 1858.

also credited St Benedict with being a key factor in the rise of Christian civilization in Europe. In his book *Religion and the Rise of Western Culture*, Dawson argued that "it was the disciplined and tireless labour of the monks which turned the tide of barbarism in Western Europe and brought back into cultivation the lands which had been deserted and depopulated in the age of the invasions."[2] Dawson was not only interested in the spiritual contribution of Benedictine monasticism but also its economic and social side-effects. Newman also drew attention to this Benedictine contribution in his *Atlantis* essay. He wrote:

> Even English, and much more foreign historians and antiquarians, have arrived at a unanimous verdict here. "We owe the agricultural restoration of great part of Europe to the monks," says Mr. Hallam. "The monks were much the best husbandmen, and the only gardeners," says Forsyth. "None," says Wharton, "ever improved their lands and possessions more than the monks, by building, cultivating, and other methods." The cultivation of Church lands, as Sharon Turner infers from the Doomsday Book, was superior to that held by other proprietors, for there was less wood upon them, less common pasture, and more abundant meadow. "Wherever they came," says Mr. Soame on Mosheim, "they converted the wilderness into a cultivated country; they pursued the breeding of cattle and agriculture, laboured with their own hands, drained morasses, and cleared away forests. By them Germany was rendered a fruitful country." M. Guizot speaks as

[2] Christopher Dawson, *Religion and the Rise of Western Europe* (New York: Image Books, 1991), 53.

strongly: "The Benedictine monks were the agri-
culturists of Europe; they cleared it on a large scale,
associating agriculture with preaching."[3]

More important than agriculture, however, is the Benedictine
contribution to scholarship. It was the monks who kept alive the
best learning of the pagan world and the teachings of the early
Church Fathers. Some of the most famous Benedictine educators
include: St Gregory the Great, St Bede the Venerable, Alcuin
of York, St Hildegard of Bingen, and St Gertrude the Great.

St Gregory the Great (c. 540–604) is a key figure in the
history of ecclesiology and in the history of monastic theology
and Church liturgy. He is also famous for sending missionaries
to convert the Anglo-Saxon tribes under the leadership of St
Augustine of Canterbury. He was a trained Roman lawyer and
administrator and a monk. His aunts Tarsilla and Æmiliana
and his mother Silvia are all saints. St Gregory's *Liber pastoralis
curae*, or book on the office of a bishop, remains a much cited
authority on this subject today.

Bede, known as the Venerable Bede (672–735), was an
English Benedictine monk in the Kingdom of Northumbria.
His most famous work, *The Ecclesiastical History of the English
People*, gained him the title "The Father of English History."
Bede also helped to establish the B C and A D dating system.
His skills as a linguist and translator were further put to use
in making the works of Early Church Fathers available to the
Anglo-Saxons in their own language.

During Bede's time the Benedictine community in Northumbria became famous as a center of learning in the liberal arts. One of its most illustrious pupils was Alcuin of York
(c. 735–804 A D). At the invitation of Charlemagne (742–814),

---

[3] Newman, "Mission of St. Benedict."

the Holy Roman Emperor, Alcuin became a leading scholar at the Carolingian court. In a letter to Charlemagne, Alcuin wrote:

> It may be that a new Athens will arise in France, and an Athens fairer than of old, for our Athens, ennobled by the teaching of Christ, will surpass the wisdom of the Academy. The old Athens had only the teachings of Plato to instruct it, yet even so it flourished by the seven liberal arts. But our Athens will be enriched by the sevenfold gifts of the Holy Spirit and will therefore surpass all the dignity of earthly wisdom.[4]

In such a manner, throughout the whole Holy Roman Empire, which in the Carolingian period included most of Western and Central Europe, Benedictine monasteries became centers of learning, foremost, of course, of theological learning, but also of the liberal arts, and of medicine.

During the Middle Ages the monasteries were the primary source of medical care because it was the monks who first maintained medical facilities such as hospitals, infirmaries, and herb gardens. Almost half of the hospitals in medieval Europe were attached to monasteries, or to priories of the Knights Hospitaller, and other religious institutions and hospices.

Besides Bede the Venerable and Alcuin of York, the British Benedictine communities also produced Sts Willibrord and Boniface. Willibrord (658–739) is known as the "Apostle to the Friesians" or the modern Dutch. He became the first bishop of Utrecht. Boniface (c. 675–754) is known as the "Apostle of the Germans."

---

[4] Letter from Alcuin to Charlemagne, cited in John Duggan, "Our Ancient Debt to Alcuin," *First Things* Web Exclusives, 10/13/17; see also: Mary Alberic, "The Better Paths of Wisdom: Alcuin's Monastic 'True Philosophy' and the Worldly Court," *Speculum* 76(4) (October, 2001): 896–910.

The Austrians were also evangelized by Benedictine monks. In this case they came from Ireland. Today in Vienna there remains the Schottenstift or, in English, Scottish Abbey, formally called *Benediktinerabtei unserer Lieben Frau zu den Schotten* (Benedictine Abbey of Our Dear Lady of the Scots). This monastery was founded in 1155 when Henry II of Austria brought Irish monks to Vienna. At this time Ireland was known in Latin as "*Scotia Major*" and Scotland was called "*Scotia Minor.*" As a consequence, in German, Irish monks were called "*Schotten*" (Scots) and the monasteries that they founded were called "*Schottenklöster.*" The Irish Benedictine monks were also involved with the foundation of the University of Vienna in 1365, and with the building of a hospice for pilgrims and crusaders, who often passed through Vienna on their way to Jerusalem.

St Hildegard was a Benedictine Abbess (1098–1179) known as "the Sibyl of the Rhine." She wrote on liturgy, music, theology, philosophy, pharmacy, and botany. She is considered to be the founder of scientific natural history in Germany. St Hildegard was proclaimed a Church Doctor by Pope Benedict XVI in 2012.

St Gertrude the Great of Helfta (1256–1302), also in Germany, is the only female saint who carries the title "the great." She went to a Cistercian school at the age of five. Cistercians are a branch of the Benedictines known for their austerity. She was a particularly intellectually gifted student who spoke of desiring to "heal the wound of ignorance." She became a mystic and wrote a number of works on spiritual conversion, reparation, preparation for death, purgatory, and devotion to the Sacred Heart. In one of her visions Our Lord told her he would release 1,000 souls from purgatory every time the following prayer is said with love and devotion: "Eternal Father, I offer you the most precious Blood of Thy divine Son, Jesus Christ, in union with the Masses said throughout the world today, for all the

Holy Souls in Purgatory, for sinners everywhere, those in the Universal Church, in my home, and in my family."

Together, Hildegard and Gertrude offer examples of influential educated Catholic womanhood centuries before anyone dreamed of the modern ideology of feminism.

So far we have mentioned that the Benedictines salvaged the best of pre-Christian classical learning, they drained swamps, established farms, built monasteries which included infirmaries for the sick, and large libraries and scriptoria for books, and their learning and charity paved the way for the development of institutions such as schools, universities, and hospitals. All of these contributions had a dramatic impact on the societies where they were present, including far flung islands in the North and Irish Seas. However their most significant contribution is that they made the liturgy, or worship, the source and summit of their whole existence.

St Teresa Benedicta of the Cross, a 20th-century martyr who was influenced by both Benedictine and Carmelite spirituality, wrote that the surrender of the soul to God is the highest achievement of its freedom. The Benedictines would agree and would add that the worship of God by the human person is the greatest act any human being can perform. This idea is often expressed in the Latin concept "Homo Orans," which describes a human person as a being made for worship. The culture of the Incarnation fostered by the Benedictines is a culture which gives priority to worship, to liturgy. In Benedictine spirituality nothing matters more than the liturgy. Time itself is sanctified through the recitation of the daily Divine Office. And since the liturgy is the summit of all human existence, the Benedictines believe that liturgies must be beautiful. The liturgical theology of Pope Benedict is deeply Benedictine, and today it is no surprise that many of the most beautiful liturgies to be experienced anywhere in the world are those offered in Benedictine monasteries.

Although St Benedict was always victorious over the devil's efforts to thwart his building plans, his successors have not been so spiritually powerful in battles with the devil. Monasteries are usually the highest targets on the hit-lists of dictators and political ideologues. When King Henry VIII had a fight with Pope Innocent VII over his divorce of Queen Katherine of Aragon, and the Pope upheld Christ's teaching on the indissolubility of marriage, Henry responded by unleashing his forces against the monasteries in the United Kingdom. The monastic treasures were looted, the buildings destroyed, the monks martyred. In the history books this is referred to as the dissolution of the monasteries. It took the form of a set of administrative and legal processes between 1536 and 1541. Professor George W. Bernard argues that the dissolution of the monasteries in the 1530s was on a revolutionary scale. He notes that prior to this time

> [t]here were nearly 900 religious houses in England, around 260 for monks, 300 for regular canons, 142 nunneries and 183 friaries; some 12,000 people in total, 4,000 monks, 3,000 canons, 3,000 friars and 2,000 nuns. If the adult male population was 500,000, that meant that one adult man in fifty was in religious orders.[5]

It was not until the 19th century that the Benedictines were allowed to re-establish themselves in the United Kingdom.

In France, the Republicans behaved the same way toward the monasteries during the period of the French Revolution. In Holland, in the 16th century Dutch Calvinists took over monasteries and turned them into workshops for Protestant tapestry weavers. After the Peace of Westphalia in Germany in 1648, Protestant Princes confiscated the lands of monastic

---

[5] George W. Bernard, *The Late Medieval Church: Vitality and Vulnerability Before the Break with Rome* (Yale University Press, 2013), 165.

orders. The same thing happened in Zurich with Protestant leaders dissolving monasteries and forcing nuns to marry. Monasteries in both Austria and Belgium was forced to close during the reign of Emperor Joseph II (1765–1790), some 500 monasteries lost their lands to the Portuguese government in the early nineteenth century, and Mexican monks were persecuted in the first half of the twentieth century. And this is far from an exhaustive list of all the political assaults on monasteries. In general, the three biggest destroyers of monasteries have been Viking raiders, Henry VIII, and French Republicans. Typically, when monasteries are closed in one part of the world, the monks move on and set up shop somewhere else.

Closer to our own times, the key figure behind the establishment of a Catholic Hierarchy in Australia was a Benedictine priest and a direct descendant of St Thomas More, William Ullathorne, who rose from being a cabin boy in the English navy to being the Archbishop of Birmingham. Among many other things he is famous for his deathbed statement that the "devil is a jackass." Ullathorne was sent to Australia (then under the ecclesial governance of the Vicar Apostolic of Mauritius) as Vicar-General in 1833. To what was then a penal colony he brought a library of some 1,000 books.

Two years later, another Benedictine, Bishop John Bede Polding OSB (1794–1877), arrived. He carried the title of Vicar Apostolic for New Holland and van Diemen's Land until his appointment as Archbishop of Sydney in 1842. In 1877, Polding was succeeded as Archbishop of Sydney by Roger Vaughan (1834–1883), a Benedictine from Downside Abbey, and younger brother of Cardinal Herbert Vaughan, Archbishop of Westminster (1832–1903). The Vaughans are an English recusant family. In Roger and Herbert's generation there were thirteen children. All five of their sisters became nuns, and six out of the eight brothers became priests, and four of the six priests became bishops. Their parents could proudly claim to be the parents of the Archbishops of Sydney and Westminster, as well as the Bishop of Menevia in Wales, and an auxiliary bishop of Salford.

It's hard to imagine any flourishing Catholic culture without the Benedictine element or Victorian Catholicism without the Vaughan family.

21

A Bucket List of Twenty Benedictine Monasteries on the Catholic Culture Tourist Trail

1. COLEBROOK, TASMANIA

Archbishop Julian Porteous has recently established a Benedictine monastery in the village of Colebrook, which is roughly an hour's drive from Hobart through a valley filled with vineyards, cellar door treats, and other gourmet and cosmetic treasures like wombat poo chocolate, Eastern Grey Kangaroo Tea, Tassie Devil chilli sauce, lemon and charcoal soap, Kakadu plum face cream and wild wallaby roasts not found on the mainland. The monastery is called Notre Dame Priory and has a website so you can check the website for details of Solemn High Masses and plan your Tassie get-away for one of the great solemnities.

2. HEILIGENKREUZ ABBEY

Heiligenkreuz is a Cistercian monastery in the village of Heiligenkreuz in the southern part of the Vienna woods. The monastery was founded in 1133 by Margrave St. Leopold III of Austria. In 1188 Leopold V of Austria presented the abbey with a relic of the True Cross which is exhibited in the chapel of the Holy Cross. This relic was a present from Baldwin IV of Jerusalem, King of Jerusalem, to Duke Leopold V in 1182. Today the Abbey is the home of the *Philosophisch-Theologische Hochschule Benedikt XVI*. This is a pontifical faculty for the study of theology and philosophy and the largest of its kind in the German-speaking world. It's a half hour taxi ride from

Vienna or 2.5 hours by train or bus. The gift shop sells liquors not found anywhere else.

3. MELK, AUSTRIA

The great Danube River originates in Germany and flows southeast for some 2,860 km passing through or touching the borders of Austria, Slovakia, Hungary, Croatia, Serbia, Romania, Bulgaria, Moldova and the Ukraine before emptying into the Black Sea. On the fertile lands surrounding its banks Benedictine monks have built some of the greatest monasteries in the world. One of these is Melk. It is easily reached by catching either a train or boat from Vienna. The tourist shops in the village beneath the monastery sell exquisitely beautiful Christian Christmas tree decorations. If you don't want to put images of Mickey Mouse and teddy bears on your tree, but angels, shepherds, miniature magi, little Bethlehem stars and so on, all very tastefully crafted, then Melk is a place to go. The abbey was founded in 1089 and is famous for its baroque architecture, especially the high altar and tabernacle, and its library. If you like Baroque, then this place has an enormous "wow factor," to borrow the jargon of real estate agents.

4. PANNONHALMA ARCHABBEY

Further along the Danube basin travelling south from Vienna, and a bus ride from the Hungarian town of Győr, there is the Archabbey of Pannonhalma. This was founded in 996 on top of a hill at the base of which it is said that Saint Martin of Tours was born. Its library includes some 360,000 volumes. It also contains a Baroque refectory and is the home of a boys' boarding school. The monks have a vineyard and they also run a restaurant for tourists. Before catching a bus to Pannonhalma one can visit the Győr Cathedral where Blessed Vilmos Apor is buried. Bishop Apor was an uncle

of Hans Urs von Balthasar. In 1945 Apor was martyred by
Soviet soldiers. He was protecting women in his palace who
were hiding from the soldiers.

5. EINSIEDELN ABBEY

Closer to home for the Balthasar family is the Benedictine
monastery in the village of Einsiedeln in the canton of Schwyz,
in Switzerland. The abbey is dedicated to Our Lady of the
Hermits, after Saint Meinrad who was a local hermit. According to legend, the church was miraculously consecrated by
Christ himself, assisted by the Four Evangelists, Saint Peter,
and Saint Gregory the Great. The Einsiedeln Monastery pos-
sesses some 250,000 volumes in its library and has a great
tradition of learning and music.

6. LE BARROUX ABBEY

Moving from Switzerland through the alpine autostrada into the
alps of France renowned for their ski-resorts, and then driving
down to Provence, one can visit the recently established monastery of Le Barroux. While much of Western civilization was
falling apart in the late 1960s, one good thing that happened
was the foundation of the Abbaye du Barroux in 1970 by Dom
Gérard Calvet, who is said to have arrived in the region on the
back of a moped looking for some place of solitude from the
general insanity of the times. For those who feel as though
one more baroque cherub will make them feel ill, Barroux is
much more austere. The monastery is famous for its splendid
liturgy, said according to the Extraordinary Form. There is also a
neighboring monastery for women. The *Domaine de Rabassière*,
located some 300 meters from the Abbaye, provides five-star
accommodation and a swimming pool for pilgrims. In the village
of Barroux itself there are some great cafes and a restaurant called
Les geraniums which has spectacular views overlooking a valley.

7. FONTGOMBAULT ABBEY

Another Extraordinary Form Abbey is the Abbey of Notre-Dame de Fontgombault located in Fontgombault in the province of Berry, France. It was founded in 1091. In the 12th and 13th centuries the abbey flourished and founded some twenty priories. In the 15th century the abbots of Fontgombault dug numerous ponds for fishing and contributed to Berry's reputation as one of the leading fishing capitals of France. The abbey was however sacked by Calvinists in 1569 and not restored until the 17th century for a brief period only. Between the 17th century and the early 20th century it was at various times used by other religious communities, sacked by republican militants, and confiscated by the French government. Its modern history goes back to 1948 when 22 monks from the great Solesmes Abbey in the Loire Valley re-founded Fontgombault as a Benedictine Abbey. It now has over 100 monks and has made three new foundations in France and one at Clear Creek in the United States. Its Abbey shop is arguably the best in France, selling not only monastery produce like honey and hand-creams, but exquisitely beautiful liturgical vessels made with gold and other precious metals. Unfortunately, they don't show-case their wares on their website, so one has to actually go to Fontgombault to stock up on First Communion and Ordination presents. Their art work, like their liturgical music, is of an extremely high standard.

8. DOWNSIDE ABBEY

For Australians interested in colonial Catholic history, the Basilica of St Gregory the Great at Downside, commonly known as Downside Abbey, in the county of Somerset, is on the "must see" list. It is the home of the English Benedictine Congregation. The community was founded in 1607 at Douai in France at a time when it was dangerous to be a Catholic in England. For nearly 200 years the monastery trained monks for the English mission; six of these men were beatified by Pope Pius XI in 1929. Two of them, Saints John Roberts and Ambrose Barlow, were among the Forty Martyrs of England and Wales canonized by Pope Paul VI in 1970. The church is built in the Gothic Revival style, and was designed to rival in size the medieval cathedrals of England that were lost to the Catholic Church because of King Henry VIII's apostasy.

9. AMPLEFORTH ABBEY

Ampleforth Abbey is in rural Yorkshire. It has been the home of a Benedictine community of monks since 1802 and it is famous for its boarding school for boys, and its beers, ciders, and brandies. It has a café for visitors and there are a couple of picture-postcard worthy English pubs in the neighboring village. It is possible to visit Ampleforth in the morning and Castle Howard in the afternoon. Castle Howard is where the ITV production of *Brideshead Revisited* was filmed.

10. FARNBOROUGH ABBEY

In 1880, the Empress Eugénie bought a house in Farnborough. Following the loss of her husband Napoleon III in 1873 and the death in 1879 of her 23-year-old son in the Zulu War, she built St Michael's Abbey as a monastery and a burial place for her husband and son. In 1895 the Empress Eugénie invited French Benedictines to take up residence in the monastery. Monsignor Ronald Knox was received into the Catholic Church here. Knox was a famous 20th-century English priest, theologian, detective story writer, and regular commentator on religious affairs for the BBC. In his memoirs he described Farnborough Abbey as "a little corner of England which is forever France, irreclaimably French." It is easily reached by a short train ride from London's Waterloo station.

11. BUCKFAST ABBEY

Another French foundation in the UK can be found near the village of Buckfastleigh in Devon. It is a day-trip from London along the very picturesque west-country rail route. Trains leave from London Paddington station and stop at Totnes. From Totnes there is the number 88 bus or alternatively, a ten-minute taxi ride. The Abbey's estate includes a guest house, a restaurant, a book shop which sells beautiful cards, a gift shop with tasteful wares, and a shop that sells produce from monasteries all over the UK. The nave of the Church is a mixture of Romanesque and Gothic styles. The Lady Chapel is exquisitely beautiful and another side chapel is the home of a hair shirt owned by St Thomas More. There is plenty of garden-space to roam around.

12. PLUSCARDEN ABBEY

Moving north to Aberdeenshire in Scotland, there is Pluscarden Abbey, founded by King Alexander II of Scotland in the year 1230. It is located near the village of Elgin, close to the North Sea. The liturgies are splendid and monastery guests are usually greeted by a gregarious black and white cat called Baxter who is missing half a tail; but one word of warning— it is *bitterly* cold in winter. It is also difficult to access by public transport. Hiring a car in Aberdeen and meandering one's way through the countryside is the best option.

13. VÉZELAY ABBEY OR BASILICA OF ST MARY MAGDALENE

Moving back across the Channel to France, in the region of Burgundy there is Vézelay Abbey. This is a must-see treasure for those interested in the Crusades and/or with a devotion to St Mary Magdalene. It was at Vézelay that St Bernard of Clairvaux called for a second crusade and Vézelay was the starting point for the Third Crusade. It was there that the armies of King

Richard the Lionheart of England and King Philip Augustus of France met and set off for the Holy Land. It is also in this basilica that one finds the relics of St Mary Magdalene. Today the Basilica is the home of the Jerusalem Community, whose vocation is to provide an oasis of prayer, silence, and peace in the "desert" of modern cities. The community was founded in the church of St Gervais in Paris in 1975. It is thus no longer a member of the Benedictine family formally speaking, but its mission is very much in line with the Benedictine devotion to sacred liturgy and the work of making beautiful liturgy.

14. THE ABBEY OF TYNIEC

Tyniec is Poland's oldest Benedictine Abbey. It is located on the Wisła River some twelve kilometers from Kraków. The first Benedictines arrived in this part of Poland in the 11th century. Throughout its long history the Abbey was taken over by military forces many times, and the current community began its life in 1939. It is possible to make a retreat here or simply do a day trip from Kraków, listen to the monks chanting the Divine Office, attend Mass, plunder the gift store, and return to Kraków. It is possible to walk to the monastery from Kraków by following the river path to the west (this takes about two hours) or for the less adventurous one can catch a river cruiser or a bus, or take a twenty-minute taxi ride. St John Paul II enjoyed visiting the monastery and did so for the last time in 2002.

15. ETTAL ABBEY

For those who like baroque and rococo architecture, Ettal Abbey in Bavaria, founded in 1330 by Emperor Ludwig the Bavarian, can be reached from the town of Oberammergau, famous for its wood carvings and Passion plays. The foundation legend is that Ludwig's horse genuflected three times on the site of the original church building. During the Second World

War the monastery was for a time the sanctuary of Dietrich Bonhoeffer, and also a place of house-arrest for the heroically anti-Nazi Jesuit priest Rupert Mayer, who was beatified by St John Paul II. The monastery maintains a Byzantine Institute as well as a brewery, distillery, bookstore, art publishing house, and a cheese factory. It is also famous for its herbal liqueur. The beers, cheeses, and liqueurs can be sampled in the monastery's beer garden.

16. OUR LADY OF CLEAR CREEK ABBEY

Our Lady of Clear Creek Abbey in the Diocese of Tulsa, Oklahoma, was founded in 1999 from the Abbey of Our Lady of Fontgombault in France. Like at the Abbey of Fontgombault, the Masses of Clear Creek Abbey are said according to the Extraordinary Form.

Getting to the Abbey in the Ozark Mountains can be difficult without a car. The nearest center is Tulsa which is some 70 miles from the Abbey. There is a family guest house where people can stay overnight and many families bring picnic lunches to share by the creek.

17. NONNBERG ABBEY

Nonnberg Abbey is a Benedictine convent in Salzburg, Austria, made famous by the movie *The Sound of Music*. It was founded by St. Rupert of Salzburg, circa 712 and has the distinction of being the oldest continually existing convent in the German-speaking world. Every morning at 6:45 am the nuns chant the morning Office. St. Erentrudis of Salzburg, first abbess of the convent, is venerated as Salzburg's patron saint. Her rock tomb is located in the crypt of the abbey's church. The convent can be reached either from the Kaigasse by climbing the Nonnbergstiege or via a lane from Nonntal.

18. THE MONASTERY OF OUR LADY OF CALVARY IN BOUZY-LA-FORÊT

This convent of Benedictine nuns is located on the edge of the forest of Orleans, ten kilometers from Saint-Benoît-sur-Loire. The main activity of the nuns apart from prayer (especially prayer for peace in the Holy Land) is the production of Eau d'Emeraude (Emerald Water), which is a bright green-colored lotion that is supposed to cure just about every skin problem and is particularly good for healing cuts and mosquito bites. The convent itself is nothing special architecturally, in fact it is quite modern, and the entrance could be to a public convenience, but if one happens to be driving around France looking for sites of Catholic cultural interest it is worthwhile pulling in here to stock up on Eau d'Emeraude.

19. ABBEY OF ST. SCHOLASTICA, SUBIACO

The Abbey of Saint Scholastica is located just outside the town of Subiaco in the Province of Rome and was founded by St Benedict. The abbey church is a Gothic building with a Romanesque-style campanile. There is also a sanctuary located a few kilometers from the abbey on the side of the mountain. Its interior is a maze of cells and chapels. The whole of the town of Subiaco is of historical and architectural interest.

Subiaco can be reached by bus from Rome. The Rome-Subiaco line is served by COTRAL, with buses departing from the Ponte Mammolo Metro B underground station (platform 7) every fifteen minutes.

20. THE ABBEY OF MONTECASSINO

Last, but far from least, there is the Abbey of Montecassino where the relics of St Benedict and his sister St Scholastica can be found under the high altar. The monastery is built on top of a mountain near the town of Cassino. It was almost completely destroyed during the Second World War but was rebuilt in the 1940s. Fortunately the relics of St Benedict and St Scholastica survived the bombing. The abbey is easily approached by car from the highway and many pilgrims travel by train from Rome to the town of Cassino. They then need to catch a bus from the train station to the abbey. Currently a bus leaving from the train station reaches the Abbey at around 10:20 am, 12:50 pm, and then at 4 pm. It leaves from the Monastery at 10:30 am, 1 pm, and 5 pm. Pilgrims should however check the bus times before embarking on any day trip from Rome because they could end up stuck at the train station staring up at the monastery from the town below but unable to actually reach it. Another warning is that from November to April the Abbey's museum is only open on Sundays. Many pilgrims also visit the Polish and British war cemeteries as a part of their day trip to the Abbey.

22

A "Top Twenty" Non-Fiction Reading List on Catholic Culture

1. Aidan Nichols, *Christendom Awake: On Re-Energising the Church in Culture* (London: T & T Clark, 1999).

2. Christopher Dawson, *Religion and Culture* (Catholic University of America Press, 2013).

3. E.I. Watkin, *Catholic Art and Culture* (London: Burns & Oates, 1942).

4. Robert Sencourt, *The Consecration of Genius* (London: Hollis & Carter, 1947).

5. Christopher Dawson, *The Making of Europe* (Catholic University of America Press, 2002).

6. Josef Pieper, *Leisure: The Basis of Culture* (San Francisco: Ignatius, 2014).

7. Joseph Ratzinger, *The Spirit of the Liturgy* (San Francisco: Ignatius, 2000).

8. James V. Schall, *Reason, Revelation and the Foundations of Political Philosophy* (Louisiana State University Press, 1987).

9. James V. Schall, *Remembering Belloc* (San Francisco: Ignatius, 2014).

10. James V. Schall, *Schall on Chesterton: Timely Essays on Timely Paradoxes* (Catholic University of America Press, 2000).

11. James V. Schall, *Another Sort of Learning* (San Francisco: Ignatius, 1988).

12. Ryan N.S. Topping, *Rebuilding Catholic Culture* (Sophia Institute, 2013).

13. Aidan Nichols, *Scattering the Seed: A Guide through Balthasar's Early Writings on Philosophy and the Arts* (Catholic University of America Press, 2006).

14. Romano Guardini, *The End of the Modern World* (Intercollegiate Studies Institute, 2001).

15. Alasdair MacIntyre, *Three Rival Versions of Moral Enquiry* (London: Duckworth, 1990).

16. Nicholas J. Healy, Jr., and D.C. Schindler, *Being Holy in the World: Theology and Culture in the Thought of David L. Schindler* (Grand Rapids: Eerdmans, 2011).

17. Aidan Nichols, *The Realm: An Unfashionable Essay on the Conversion of England* (Oxford: Family Publications, 2008).

18. Stratford Caldecott, *Beauty for Truth's Sake: On the Re-enchantment of Education* (Brazos Press, 2017).

19. Stratford Caldecott, *The Power of the Ring: The Spiritual Vision Behind* The Lord of the Rings *and* The Hobbit (Crossroad Publishing, 2012).

20. James and Joanna Bogle, *A Heart for Europe* (London: Gracewing, 2000).

TRACEY ROWLAND HOLDS THE ST. JOHN
Paul II Chair of Theology at the University of Notre Dame
(Australia) and is an Honorary Fellow of Campion College (Sydney) and a member of the International Theological Commission. From 2001 to 2017 she was the Dean of the John Paul II Institute for Marriage and Family (Melbourne).

Made in the USA
Las Vegas, NV
12 December 2023

82575084R00104